PLAYHOUSE

OPTIMISTIC STORIES OF REAL HOPE FOR FAMI-
LIES WITH LITTLE CHILDREN

D1319588

PLAYHOUSE: OPTIMISTIC STORIES OF REAL HOPE FOR FAMILIES WITH LITTLE CHILDREN

MONICA TAYLOR

GARN PRESS
NEW YORK, NY

Published by Garn Press, LLC
New York, NY
www.garnpress.com

Book and cover design by Benjamin J. Taylor/Garn Press
Cover images of children by Arefyeva Victoria, used under license from Shutterstock
Cover watercolor images of landscape, sky, building, tree, and balloon by ArtMosfera, used under license from Envato

Library of Congress Control Number: 2017946122

Publisher's Cataloging-in-Publication Data

Names: Taylor, Monica
Title: Playhouse : optimistic stories of real hope for families with little children / Monica Taylor.
Description: Includes bibliographical references.
Identifiers: Identifiers: LCCN 2017946122 | ISBN 978-1-942146-66-7 (pbk.) | ISBN 978-1-942146-69-8 (hardcover) | ISBN 978-1-942146-60-5 (ebook)
Subjects: LCSH: Education--Parent participation. | Progressive education. | Early childhood education--Activity programs. | Empathy in children. | Interpersonal relations in children. | Social justice. | BISAC: EDUCATION / Early Childhood. | EDUCATION / Parent Participation. | EDUCATION / Aims & Objectives. | EDUCATION / Multicultural Education. | FAMILY & RELATIONSHIPS / Education.
Classification: LCC LB1139.35.A37.T45 2017 (print) | LCC LB1139.35.A37 (ebook) | DDC 371.5--dc23.
LC record available at https://lccn.loc.gov/2017946122.

To Nanny who taught me how to love …

To Jeanne who taught me to embrace struggle …

To Maria who taught me to appreciate each individual child …

Contents

ACKNOWLEDGEMENTS

Every so often you come across a love project, an endeavor that you have to take on even if you are unsure how. Writing this book about Playhouse really has been that project for me. When Michael was in his third year at Playhouse, my grandmother passed away and it completely devastated me. She was my shelter and my lifeline from the time I was a little child. I felt unanchored and a little lost. At about that same time, I became co-president of Playhouse and found myself spending more and more time there. Who knew that Playhouse and in particular Jeanne would become another touchstone for me? Jeanne is an incredibly special and unique person – small, unassuming, yet observant and so full of love – everything that she says feels profound but also livable. Sheila Gallanter said that parents listen to Jeanne as if they were at church and I totally understand what she means. Jeanne is a sage, guide, or even guru – and yet she is the most human and accessible person you will ever meet. I am forever grateful for my time spent with Jeanne and the many lessons she has taught me as a mother, a teacher, and a woman.

While I was co-president, as a community we began to worry about how to ensure that the Playhouse philosophy remain intact, present, and alive in the school. With that goal in mind, Jeanne, Anat and Lisa, the school directors, and I began to write the *Pillars of Playhouse* (2006) together. It was in writing the pillars that I had a chance to connect with Jeanne and really get to know her and the Playhouse story. Later she arranged for me to interview several of the founding parents as well as many other families and teachers. I am grateful to each and every person who was willing to take the time to share their love of Playhouse and their optimistic and hopeful stories. I would also like to thank Anat and Lisa, both former Playhouse parents, for their ongoing support and faith that somehow I would find the right home for this book.

I extend my gratitude to the Playhouse teachers as well, in particular Maria, Danielle, and Laura, who always welcomed my boys into their classrooms with a smile and a huge hug. There were many afternoons when Michael and Griffin just did not want to leave their beloved friends at Playhouse.

Next I would like to thank my boys, Michael and Griffin, both because they led me to Playhouse but also because they have helped me to become the mother, teacher, and activist that I am today. I so appreciate that they have allowed me to share their stories in this book even if some are a little embarrassing, and that they have grown into interesting, thoughtful, creative, kind, and very funny young men. Of course I would be remiss if I did not also acknowledge the love and support that Mark has provided me throughout the time I researched and wrote this book.

Additionally, I want to thank Alice Peck who during my early years of work on the book served as a kind and gentle writing coach who guided me in writing from my heart and not just my mind. Bridget Looney, my doctoral assistant, was invaluable too as she helped to format and edit the text.

Finally, I want to thank Denny Taylor, my amazing publisher, academic mother and mentor, and Garn Press. I took my first doctoral course with Denny when she was a visiting professor at the University of Arizona where she was ethnographically researching Ken and Yetta Goodman. In many ways she taught me much of what I know about being a researcher and writer. When I met with Denny a couple of years ago I told her how frustrated I was feeling about not finding the right home for my Playhouse book. Unlike many of the other publishers to whom I had spoken, when I told Denny about my idea for the book – of writing from my perspective of a mother who is also an academic and illustrating the school through the stories of children and families – she immediately saw the magic and offered me a contract. Thank you Denny for believing in children and progressive schools and supporting families to find and create spaces where children can imagine.

AUTHOR'S NOTE

As I stated in the acknowledgements, this book has been a labor of love but it has also been a rather long term project spanning eleven years. The idea for the book emerged organically as so often is the case with my writing. Initially in 2005, as co-president of Playhouse, I worked with Jeanne and Anat to write the school's mission statement. Nothing like that had been written before and the Playhouse Board was concerned that we needed a document to maintain the integrity of the philosophy of the school. Jeanne, Anat, and I spent hours working on the mission statement, which eventually became the *Pillars of Playhouse* (2006), a pamphlet which is given to new families when they come to Playhouse. Throughout the book this pamphlet is referenced.

It was during those writing work sessions that I felt like there was a story to be told about Playhouse. Without a real plan in place, in 2006, I asked Jeanne if I could formally interview her. Over several months, we met regularly and I audio-recorded our conversations. These somewhat loose interviews sparked the idea of wanting to invite other founding parents who were local and available to meet and speak with me. Because Jeanne was still in touch with many of the families she helped me to schedule the interviews. We invited former parents and sometimes former students to the school, and together Jeanne and I would ask them questions about their memories of Playhouse. Often Jeanne and those interviewed would reconstruct the details of a memory together. Other times Jeanne and I traveled to visit Playhouse families or I interviewed them on the telephone. In 2009, I helped to organize Jeanne's 90th birthday party and we invited families from 1951 to the present. As part of the invitation, we asked people to share stories about Jeanne and Playhouse. This provided me with another sources of stories. I had the good fortune of interviewing a total of 23 former Playhouse families who attended the school from the years 1951 until the 1990s. The quotes used throughout the book provide a rich descriptive lens and include a variety of voices from these transcribed interviews.

Additionally, I used the stories of my own children's experiences which I had very roughly recorded in a journal during the years 2002-2008. I thought that telling my children's stories would provide tangible examples for readers. In order to provide a complex and honest portrait of the school, I attempted to weave together narratives from the interviews with the stories of my children. I also spent some time observing in all of the school's classrooms so that I would be able to describe a coherent picture of the school, and I met with several teachers informally to hear their perspectives about teaching at Playhouse. Finally, Anat provided me with access to the school's historical documents as well as photo albums. This helped to round out narratives that needed more detail.

Eleven years later I am so grateful to all of the families, alumni, teachers, and students who were willing to speak with me about their love of Playhouse and its impact on their lives. And most of all I am grateful to having spent all of those many years with Jeanne. This is her story as much as it is Playhouse's.

CHAPTER 1

PLAYHOUSE
AN INTRODUCTION

Pete Seeger once said (Seeger quotes, 2014): "The key to the future of the world is finding the optimistic stories and letting them be known." In many ways, writing a book about my family's experiences at Playhouse, a cooperative pre-school founded in 1951, is in fact telling an optimistic story that has the potential to inspire others, early childhood teachers and parents alike, to search for, create, or contribute to progressive learning environments both for their own children and other students. This optimistic telling serves as a reminder for us all that even in this tumultuous storm of standards and testing, progressive preschools with deep commitments to social justice exist, are thriving, and are available.

The first really hard decision most parents have to make – soon after getting rid of diapers and bottles, but long before deciding when children can walk to the playground by themselves – is where to send their children to preschool. The available information is both daunting and overwhelming. From Amy Chua's notion of Tiger Mothers (2011) to *Race to Nowhere* – the documentary which highlighted how much pressure our kids are really under – from concerns about stress and the mental health of our children to the current Opt-Out movement and other means through which parents are advocating for their kids, and in a world where all parents are rightly or wrongly told they should aspire to propel their children toward Harvard and are accused of being helicopter parents, choosing the right preschool has become the first step to children growing up to be happy and intelligent people. Parents receive mixed messages about what their expectations should be of a preschool education, and this leaves them feeling frustrated and confused about selecting preschools for their children.

There are lots of factors to consider during the process, from location and transportation to what's available in a community to address learning needs, but the most important questions to ask are what educational principles are valued, and ultimately what sort of educational foundation will be built for the child? How will what they do at three years old impact who they will be when they grow up? How will they learn to be persistent and focused individuals who have confidence and strong communication skills? How will they learn to develop a life that is both fulfilling and stimulating, a path that is true to their own interests and needs? Where can a parent turn for guidance or more information?

Beyond the parent perspective, early childhood educators themselves feel confused and often frustrated by the pressures of federal government policies like No Child Left Behind and Race to the Top. They feel they are being forced to focus on skills and drills in the hopes of meeting such criteria as the Common Core Standards. As Kohn explained in *The New York Times Sunday*

Review (May 16th, 2015):

> Twenty years ago, kids in preschool, kindergarten and even first and second grade spent much of their time playing: building with blocks, drawing or creating imaginary worlds, in their own heads or with classmates. But increasingly, these activities are being abandoned for the teacher-led, didactic instruction typically used in higher grades.

Interestingly, much of the research suggests that starting to focus on traditional academics early does not in fact lead to more productive learners in elementary school and beyond. It actually has the completely opposite effect. Young children need time to play, ask authentic questions, explore materials, and create. Ultimately college and employment readiness involves the types of skills that play and imagination foster – to be creative and innovative, to think critically, to analyze and solve problems, to apply knowledge and ideas to the real world, and to have an awareness of others beyond the United States.

My Journey to Playhouse

This book is my story of Playhouse – told from my perspective as both a parent and a teacher educator – and of grappling to figure out what was best for my children when they were preschool age from the years 2002-2008. Progressive, socially just education is in my bones – it is an embodied commitment that was deeply planted in me as a child. I spent much of my early childhood with my grandmother, Nanny, a progressive kindergarten teacher in the Bronx, who was greatly influenced by the educational philosophy of John Dewey. Funnily her best friend Gert was actually Dewey's secretary at Teachers College, and so when I mentioned to her that

I was reading Dewey's *Experience and Education* (1938) in my first Masters level teacher education course, she chuckled and said, "Oh Dewey. His theories were easy to apply. It was all about learning through doing! My kindergarten classes were all about experiencing." Nanny modeled what an emergent inquiry based curriculum looked like in all my daily interactions with her. Every activity, including unloading the dishwasher, making the beds, doing the grocery shopping, and preparing meals, had some educational purpose. You could say that she parented or grand-parented that way. Everything we did together felt fun, interesting, important, and filled with love. There was so much to talk about, question, read, and explore. What felt like her undivided attention to my needs made me feel valued and worthwhile.

This was not only modeled in our day to day exchanges. I also spent many days in her classroom. Nowadays this would never be permitted, but in those days the administrators did not mind my being at PS 83 in the Northeastern part of the Bronx. This was a great relief for my divorced working mom on my off days from private school. I realize now what a luxury this was for my mother, rather than scrambling to find childcare like so many working parents today. Even though I wasn't much older than the children in the class, Nanny expected me to assist her in any way that I could. She asked me to prep the peg boards, set out the crayons, cut out shapes for the children, tidy up the different learning centers – like the block area or the dress up corner – or prepare the snack by placing several crackers on a napkin and pouring juice into little cups. I also know, looking back, that many of these types of pedagogical experiences are no longer acceptable in the kindergarten classroom. Nanny knew that my assisting her in the classroom would be its own form of learning and that she was creating another scaffold for her own students. In those days, there were two sections of kindergarten: a morning class and an afternoon class. I believe that public schools all over the country, including Verona where we live, continue to offer families half day kindergartens because kindergarten is not considered compulsory. This creates another interesting dilemma for families with two working parents.

Part of my assisting Nanny also meant participating in any informal meetings with her colleagues. This included lunch time when I always felt so grown up and special as I sat with the teachers and talked about teaching activities or individual students. I loved every minute of my time as a "teacher" in her class, and those early years laid the foundation for my own progressive beliefs about teaching and learning.

Although teaching was such a part of my upbringing, when the time came to decide what I wanted to be when I grew up, I was resistant to the education profession. I am sure that the lack of glamour as well as society's negative perspective of teaching did not help. But, when push came to shove and my parents were pressuring me to commit to something, I decided that the only thing I really did know about myself was that I did have some teaching ability. Because the world is very small and there are only six degrees of separation, I actually got my first job because of Nanny. Spending all of that time at PS 83 as a little girl was an excellent way of self-promotion. At the wee age of 8, the principal there told Nanny to let her know if I ever decided to become a teacher because she promised to give me my first job. Fast forward 13 years, and after graduating from college, I indeed decided to become a teacher – especially if I could live and teach in NYC. Nanny's principal had long since retired, and her replacement principal, who knew my grandmother because she substitute taught after retirement in her school, had been promoted to Assistant Superintendent of District 3 in Manhattan. Nanny called him up and asked if he would consider hiring me. With no teacher credentials, and a Bachelors of Arts in French and Italian, he made it clear that I was pretty much on the bottom of the hiring totem pole but with a foreign language emergency certification I might just get a job. And three weeks later, on a Saturday morning, I was hired to teach Spanish and French at an alternative middle school in Manhattan. Yes – you heard correctly – Spanish, a subject which I had studied extensively in high school but had not spoken much in college. I jumped at the job although I had no real teaching experience or formal training.

Although only for a short time in my life, those years of working in Nanny's kindergarten class as well as the ways in which she grand-parented me came back to me during my first year of teaching. I am not going to pretend that it wasn't an extremely challenging year on a lot of levels – but I also grew tremendously and my eyes were opened to a whole other New York City – one that was culturally vibrant, racially and socioeconomically diverse, and troubled by so many social inequities. I began taking courses at City College of New York in my second year of teaching, and although I was still feeling very overwhelmed, I was fortunate to have an incredibly inspiring professor, Cindy Onore, who supported my initial exploration of progressive teaching beliefs. Being first introduced to Dewey, Freire, and Vygotsky, I was immersed in complex theories that I did not completely understand, but they seemed to resonate with my teaching instincts. I tried to facilitate learning that was authentic, student centered, and experiential. I understood from my own history of being a language learner immersed in diverse language settings (besides attending a bilingual French school in my early years, I also lived abroad for four years in France, England, Greece, and Bahrain), that the only way to learn language was to use it for real meaning making. I taught for five years but feeling like I was not making enough change, I pursued a PhD in language, reading, and culture, which gave me a stronger theoretical understanding of learning and development, but no concrete experience.

Several years later I found myself in my new life, starting a new career as a professor of teacher education, married, and the mother of a young child. In my first year of teaching at Montclair State University, untenured, sleep deprived, and searching for a preschool, I had a strong sense of the kinds of learning experiences I hoped for Michael, my oldest and at the time my only child, but I did not necessarily know how to find them. As strange as it may sound considering I have a PhD in education, I felt like my theoretical background did not adequately prepare me to make educational decisions for Michael, my real live child who was exciting, smart, and engaging, but also quirky, unpredictable, and well yes my first baby. I felt completely overwhelmed by the task of finding the right place for him. And the pressure went beyond simply finding the perfect educational space for him. I was also looking for a school that could accommodate my work schedule, because I had hoped that I could save the cost of my babysitter to pay for preschool tuition. Where could I find a preschool that both provided the progressive learning environment that I at least thought I wanted for Michael, which also had flexible hours and an understanding of the dynamics of working families? These were the philosophical and practical tensions of which I was trying to make sense.

It may sound as if I had an advantageous perspective on making decisions about Michael's preschool, but from the conversations I was having with my other mother friends, it was clear that we were all struggling to decide what our options were and how we were going to juggle our commitments as either working or stay at home mothers. We were looking for schools that would resemble the parenting principles that we used at home, but for many of us as first time parents we were not even clear what these tenets were. We all had different needs and concerns and we were struggling to find the right fit.

Truth be told, when I stumbled upon Playhouse through a word of mouth recommendation, which is THE primary way in which Playhouse but also most cooperative schools recruit families, I knew I had found the right school for our family. My son Michael was only 18 months old when I began my search. The minute I entered Playhouse I knew that it would be a fit for us. Marybeth, the educational director at the time, greeted me at the door with a welcoming smile. She invited me to sit with her and then spent over 30 minutes sharing Playhouse's philosophy. In those 30 minutes, I got the sense that the school's relationship with the parents was important. As she discussed the "open-door" policy for families, the valuing of the individual learner, the focus on learning through play and a child-centered curriculum, the promotion of compassion and peace, and the commitment to teaching emergent literacy practices rather than drilling the alphabet and numbers, I began to breathe. Could it be possible that I had found the perfect school community? I had only visited one other preschool but I knew within 3 minutes of my visit there that it was not the place for my child. As we later toured Playhouse and met Jeanne Ginsberg, one of its founders, I knew I was making the right decision. Both of my sons, Michael, now 16, and Griffin, 13, attended Playhouse for 3 years each. So different in demeanor and interests, each child felt loved, nurtured, and accepted at Playhouse. Their teachers quickly realized their strengths, needs, and interests, and strove to differentiate instruction based on their uniqueness as learners, members of a family, and people. Each child grew to develop a strong sense of self, a constant thirst to discover, and an ability to clearly articulate feelings and thoughts.

My arrival at Playhouse marked fifty years since Jeanne Ginsburg and the founding families had started the school. After meeting the directors and taking a tour of the school, I knew almost immediately that it was the perfect place for my family. It promised to allow me to bridge my academic expertise with my life experience as a grandchild first and later a parent. I hoped that Michael and later Griffin would have the opportunities to experience a child-centered socially-just curriculum founded in inquiry-based teaching. I wanted my children to be invited to think critically and be encouraged to develop as thoughtful, inquisitive, self-reflective, and creative citizens and problem-solvers. These were the philosophical commitments of Playhouse.

Why Write about Playhouse?

Playhouse serves as more than just a school for children. It is a learning community for parents, where they can learn and embrace progressive models of education. This type of parental education is more important now than ever before, especially in the context of parental opt out movements and objections to standardized testing and curriculum like the common core standards. Parents and early childhood teachers need to educate themselves about the tenets of democratic and progressive schooling, and while there is little new writing for them, the books by Nelson (2016) and Fine (2015) are the exceptions. Most of what is out there is geared toward academics. My contemporaries, parents and teachers, who are in their thirties and forties and who grew up in the '70s and '80s recall their own progressive schooling experiences, but are not sure what options they have for their own children, especially since technology has given us so many choices. Early childhood teachers often graduate with certification but are unsure of how to implement this progressive pedagogy in their classrooms or how even to find schools where these types of practices are encouraged. They may have been prepared to teach in a progressive way but are unsure of how to apply these ideas in the classroom with 15 or more little ones in front of them. Progressive teaching is incredibly rewarding but can also be challenging to operationalize. This is especially true if the teachers are committed to developing child centered curriculum. Finally, with the Common Core Curriculum Standards and their aligned standardized tests dictating the curriculum and teaching in public schools, parents and early childhood educators need a platform to innovate schools for their children/students.

As documentaries like the runaway grassroots hits *Waiting for "Superman"* and *Race to Nowhere* and people like Diane Ravitch and Ken Robinson point out, success in our present educational culture is wrongly beginning to be defined as producing high standardized test scorers rather than cultivating creative, compassionate, and innovative problem-solvers. In describing the Playhouse experience, I give parents and early childhood educators insights into alternative ways of thinking about schools, where they begin to focus on the whole child and where they recognize a viable way for parents and teachers to work together in the best interests of the child. This book provides the philosophical tenets of progressive teaching in an accessible and tangible manner. It also highlights the strategies that not only facilitate navigating the preschool/childcare experience but also apply to all aspects of early childhood teaching. Through the stories of Playhouse, I illustrate the tenets and signs of a good, progressive preschool that provides an environment that nurtures creative and compassionate beings.

Just as Playhouse helped me to blend my own theoretical knowledge with my life experiences, this book will make progressive early childhood learning and teaching more accessible to parents and teachers. The story of Playhouse is told through the integration of the beliefs and practices of the school with my own personal narratives of my grandmother and my children, as well as stories from other teachers, former Playhouse parents and children, and most importantly Jeanne Ginsburg, the educational founding director of Playhouse.

Seeger and Ginsburg: Progressive Educators

This land is your land, this land is my land
From California to the New York Island
From the Redwood Forest to the Gulf Stream waters
This land was made for you and me. (Guthrie, 1945)

If you were raised in the 70s, these song lyrics may take you on a nostalgic journey through time to your own kindergarten or first grade classroom when you were sitting, cross legged (what is now called crisscross apple sauce), in a circle on the rug, singing "This land is your land." Can you remember the way you felt when you were singing this song? Did you feel like you belonged to something? Did you feel hopeful? I actually think I have more memories of singing this song than I do of singing the national anthem or even saying the Pledge of Allegiance. I believed, even if writing it now makes me think I was pretty naïve, that these lyrics represented a new United States, one that was inclusive, compassionate, open minded, and peaceful. And although Woody Guthrie wrote the song, I think for many of us we associate the lyrics with Pete Seeger. Can't you hear the banjo chords and his distinct raspy voice singing the lyrics?

Now why would I engage you in this walk down memory lane? What does Pete Seeger have to do with progressive education, cooperative preschools, Playhouse, or even Jeanne Ginsburg? Two summers ago, I took my boys to our annual "hippie fest" – or at least that is what they affectionately call the Clearwater Revival Festival. It is a festival that emerged from the Clearwater grassroots organization that Pete Seeger and his wife Toshi started in 1969 as a way to clean up the Hudson River. Clearwater aspires to inspire, educate, and activate generations of people to preserve and protect the Earth. Its mission is to "support growing grass-roots efforts and provide educational experiences to all people, especially youth of various ethnicities, economic and cultural backgrounds, to help new generations of strong environmental stewards."

One afternoon while we were enjoying a band at the main stage, a torrential rainstorm emerged and we ran under a gazebo to find shelter. Of course about 30 or so other people did the same thing and we all sat under the gazebo while we waited for the rain to pass. As people chatted, shared food, improvised on instruments, and even broke out in song, it was a wonderful opportunity to take a good look at the Clearwater population and reflect on what this community represents and why it is so heartwarming. As I looked around, I also felt a moment of sadness as I was reminded of Pete Seeger's death a year prior (Pareles, 2014) as well as the aging of those in the community. On the bright side I was optimistic as I looked around to see how many young families were present and I wondered how we would find ways to sustain a commitment to social justice, peace and compassion, and environmental sustainability that was the mission of the Pete Seeger generation.

Pete Seeger believed "in the power of community – to stand up for what's right, speak out against what's wrong, and move this country closer to the America he knew we could be." Over the years, he used his voice – and his hammer – to strike blows for worker's rights and civil rights, for world peace and environmental conservation. And he always invited us to "sing along" (Obama's Statement of the President, 2014). Thinking about both this moment in time as well as my eight years at Playhouse, I began to consider the ways in which Pete Seeger and the founders of Playhouse shared a similar progressive worldview, how their shared beliefs about social justice, activism, and teaching and learning, and how these were the very values that drew me to them. After all, folk music provided an access to more authentic cultural resources – a whole range of unique narratives that illustrated the diversity of the human experience rather than the canned historical tales that we often tell children. In addition, folk music is described as the "early experiences of democratic attitudes and values" (Crawford-Seeger, 1948, p. 22) because of the ways in which it crosses boundaries and invites people to participate and improvise. Even more interesting is a deeper connection between Pete Seeger and Playhouse of which I was not aware until sometime into my research about cooperative preschools in the 1950s. Pete Seeger's stepmother, Ruth Crawford-Seeger, was the music director and a mother at the Silver Springs Co-op School, a significant model of cooperative schools at the time and one that greatly influenced Playhouse.

Folk music welcomes individual expression within a democratic community, very much what I had hoped my own children would experience in preschool. I was looking for a place where my children would be valued as individuals, where there was a deep commitment to social justice, and where they would be encouraged to experience the natural world as a site of inquiry. Playhouse, its philosophy, and its leadership and guidance through Jeanne Ginsburg were familiar and comforting to me and were the perfect fit for my family.

Meet Jeanne Ginsburg: The Heartbeat of Playhouse

I have an insatiable curiosity of what makes people tick, big people and little people, and I always felt that when I put my emphasis on why is this happening, what is underneath it, looking for some kind of root instead of just treating a symptom, I felt I was able to work with it in a positive way. What I think a teacher does is sow seeds into children that they're working with. You plant the seeds, and you nurture them, and if you create the right environment, a healthy environment, they'll grow. (Jeanne Ginsburg, Playhouse Video)

Just like Pete Seeger, Jeanne Ginsburg was born in 1919. She grew up in Newark, NJ and graduated from Weequahic High School in 1937. Like many adults who came of age during the Depression and "the war years" there was no money for her to go to college, so she worked in New York with her family for about ten years. In 1944, feeling like she had a lot of time on her hands and looking for things to stimulate her, Jeanne enrolled in a workshop at Goddard College in Vermont on economics and labor relations. The lectures and the conversations she had with other participants introduced her to a different social way of life that was not just driven by profits.

She reflected: "Here were people discussing ideas – just better ways of living so that everyone could benefit and a better way of living that appealed to me so. It motivated me to start reading more … I read different theories on styles of life and governing." The following summer she spent six weeks at the University of New Hampshire and took several courses including government and politics, art appreciation, and golf. Encouraged by some of her new friends, she enrolled at the University of Colorado at Boulder the summer after. It was there that she decided that she wanted to be a kindergarten teacher. This is Jeanne's retelling of that decision:

> The day before we enrolled in classes, we were just getting into our dorms and getting acclimated, I was walking into town by myself – I didn't know anybody. I heard two women behind me sort of talking a little louder, obviously wanting me to hear them and I heard one of them say, "I bet you she's a kindergarten teacher." And the other said, "I bet she teaches …" But when she said kindergarten teacher, and I knew she meant me because there was no one else on the street, I turned around and they smiled and I smiled. They said, "Are you?" And I said, "No but it sounds good." You know I thought it appealed to me. So we started walking into town together and talking. And the next day, when we registered, I registered for a course in early childhood growth and development.

It was actually not as simple as she thought. She wasn't matriculated into a program and this course was a prerequisite, but she was able to convince the professor to let her take the course. That was the beginning of a long journey into becoming an early childhood educator. Taking the course reminded her that she had always been interested in children. Returning back home that fall, she began a new life working as an assistant teacher for her friend May Berger at the Young Men's Hebrew Association (YMHA) preschool in the morning, her family's business in the afternoon, and going to NYU at night to get her degree. She studied recreation education at NYU, not early childhood education, but her experiences at the YMHA laid the foundation for her beliefs about teaching young children. As she recalled, "I had good training under May. What she did with me, as assistant, whenever she had the group, the non-conformers who were always disrupting the class, she would put me with them. I had to take care of the difficult ones so she could have the group. I really learned a lot. I just had to pull things out of the hat and try to calm these kids down."

Jeanne did some of her fieldwork at a public school in NYC. It was then that she feels she really learned about listening to and observing kids. She was required to interview children and these are her reflections about the experience:

> I had to take them out one by one and just engage in conversation, find out what they worried about. I found out a lot about kids, how important it was to open them up and how to listen to them. I was just forced into it. There wasn't any guide to tell me what to do. They just said, "Talk to them." So I talked to them. They were eager to open up. I discovered that you just had to ask them a question or two and just stop and listen and kids would open up to you. That's what I did.

> I learned there were kids from broken homes, what they worried about. They had a lot on their minds, heavy problems, family problems that they usually heard their parents discuss at night when they thought they were sleeping. At night, when they were in bed they could hear big discussions going on. Kids carry a lot of that with them even to school. They would talk about big heavy problems. I can even remember to this day this kid saying, "I'm a worry to my mother. I worry her." And I said, "How can you tell that?" and he said, "When she thinks I'm sleeping I hear her talk."

Founding Playhouse

> It was the era where everybody was into having children. It was post-war. The idea was a kind of togetherness. It gave us a challenge to be doing things for our children but it was also an intellectual and social outlet … We were kind of social activists from the beginning … wanting to change society. (Gloria Steiner, Founder of Playhouse)

In particular, a group of parents and Jeanne Ginsburg decided to open Playhouse, a progressive cooperative preschool. The original parents group included Gloria and Charlie Steiner, Carol and Sanford Lewis, Barbara and Buddy Schiller, Randy Stiles, and Carolyn and David Rothschild. They wanted to create an alternative educational experience for their children based on the ideals of cooperative schools, child-centered classrooms, hands-on learning and caring, compassion and social justice. Jeanne considered the founding mothers radicals, liberals, and very democratic, who were all committed to social justice and more than willing and able to fight for justice. Jeanne gave this story as an example:

> Another woman, Dee Henneke … was a firecracker. She was probably at the lead of wanting to get [Playhouse] diverse. Course, she stuck her neck out. There used to be swim clubs in the area then that she would join with her kids in the summer … And I remember one of the top-notch upper income swim clubs, she joined there and she wanted to have a friend who was African-American. They wouldn't let her, and she just did it, and they stopped her, and she left, she withdrew her membership. I mean she was right there, she followed with everything she believed, what a woman… She was not just a talker, she was a doer… She

was a radical before her time.

The 1930s to the 1950s brought a surge of new cooperative schools around the United States. These cooperatives were created for multiple reasons. The period immediately following the war seemed to encourage a unique group of middle class mothers who felt conflicted about their next life steps. Having completed a college degree, they felt compelled to do something for the greater public good, but on the other hand they were committed to facilitating a rich family life. These conflicting pressures encouraged women to create cooperative preschools where they could focus on child rearing, but also participate in a democratic organization that served the needs of other families. Being involved in these schools enabled women to avoid what Betty Friedan (1963) later called "the problem that has no name" (p. 15), a problem that was rampant among many isolated suburban mothers. Suburban housewives felt alone and dissatisfied with their lives yet they were too afraid to say anything about it.

These new democratic cooperative schools provided them with opportunities to exercise shared decision making (Muncy, 2004). Any democratic endeavor was also welcomed because of the aftermath of the war and the re-commitment to democracies rather than totalitarian regimes. Additionally because many families moved to the suburbs, they were looking for community, or for an extended family to which they and their children could belong (Hewes, 1998). From the beginning, the founders of Playhouse understood the important connections between family and school life. They wanted to be involved in their children's early experiences and to have a school where their moral values were reflected.

Jeanne was recruited as the main teacher from the conception of the school and later became the educational director. In her words:

> I heard about this group of women planning to start a
> co-op the year I was about to get my degree from New York
> University. I had a friend who knew them through The
> American Jewish Congress ... They wanted a co-op where
> they could be part of the program and learn along with the
> children ... I had heard of economic co-ops. And I liked the
> idea behind the philosophy of a group of people working
> together common goal. I studied about them in Scandinavia
> ... The co-op immediately sparked this interest in me and
> I thought, well, applying it to young children, who I had
> be trained to work with – what a wonderful combination.

Jeanne's original plan had been to get her degree and then teach in Newark with low income children – another connection that Jeanne and I have as much of my work has been around urban education and in Newark. She shared that plan with the founding parents who explained that they too had a social justice mission, and that they should combine their interests and work together to start Playhouse. As Jeanne recalled:

> And they said, why don't you come and stay with us. We
> believe in that too. So there was a meeting of minds then,
> that's how it was. They said don't go to Newark, we'll do it
> here. That's how it was.

Jeanne and the founding parents developed the structure of Playhouse from a variety of different sources. They visited the Silver Spring Cooperative Nursery School, a well-known model cooperative school in Silver Springs, Maryland, which published handbooks, curricula, and other publications to illustrate the principles and operations of a cooperative school. The Playhouse families hoped to base their school on the same principles. They asked Carolyn Rothschild, one of the founding parents, to share expertise drawing from her Masters from Cornell in early childhood education. However, more than any other resource they greatly relied on Jeanne and her deep understandings of young children. Very simply put, Jeanne understood that building relationships with parents was the key to working with young children. She reflected: "I always felt from the very beginning that you couldn't do much good with a child unless you reached their parents at the same time." This became the guiding principle at Playhouse.

The school began in 1951 with ten middle class families who had children between the ages of three and four. It was housed at 181 Academy St. in South Orange, in a Hebrew school they rented. Five new families joined the group, including Dee and Art Henecke, Lola Silver, who was the first president of Playhouse, Dottie and Lenny Tyler, Dina and Ted Cohen, and Ed Bowzer and his wife, an African-American architect who later built the Playhouse building. Originally Playhouse offered a half day of school, during which time two parents and Jeanne were the instructors. This of course meant that all parents were required to cooperate with or assist the teacher, one day a week. The fathers were equally involved in the school as the mothers, and attended the monthly Board meetings and volunteered to carpool as well as other jobs. They also initiated Maintenance Day, which they still have to this day, where parents would come in on the weekends to repair and clean the school. They primarily were able to fund the school through tuitions but they also received some donations from the community. They also implemented a tuition sliding scale, so that how much tuition a family paid was based on their income.

From that first year, this was a way to operationalize their belief of the importance of attracting a diverse school population. They wanted all families to have access to the school, and they valued the idea of having children and families from different racial, religious, and economic backgrounds. The school was not elaborate or fancy. There was a milk wagon in the back-yard from a dairy farm in Roseland, a swing, and a sandbox, and the classroom was very bare bones – there were easels, puzzles, books, records and a record player, a piano, and wooden blocks. And although they appreciated the use of the space they were renting, from the get go they dreamt of having their own school building. Today Playhouse, accommodating the needs of families in which two parents work, has a variety of options for children's classes, ranging from all day school which begins at 7:30 am and goes until 5:30 pm, as well as shortened morning programs that are only from 9:00 am to 11:00 am.

Nurturing a Home-School Partnership

The founders of Playhouse and specifically Jeanne understood the importance of a true home-school partnership. To nurture this partnership, Playhouse teachers value the "funds of knowledge" (Moll, Amanti, Neff, & Gonzalez, 1992) of families and find many opportunities to build from these in the classroom. Because of this framework, the children see continuity between their home and school. They realize that who they are, how they speak, and what cultural values and interests they have, are all accepted in school.

Building from a progressive education foundation informed by Dorothy Baruch (1939) and Arnold Gesell (Gesell & Ilg, 1949), the school considered itself a place to engage children as democratic citizens. The classrooms became communal spaces where children experienced the notion of "equality" and practiced negotiating, sharing, and taking turns. They experienced the division of "community responsibilities," and "acquired tolerance by observing differences among their peers" (Baruch, 1939, p. 206). Children learned to use talk to settle differences, having a chance "to defend their own rights and to recognize the rights of others" (Baruch, 1939). This is similar to the approach of the Downtown Alternative School described by Fine (2015). Playhouse teachers understood "how important it is for children to experience the power that language gives them in effectively getting themselves across to others" (p. 210). In the school, "the rules by which [everyone] lives will be mutually understood and cooperatively developed – the way democratic peoples have always worked out their rules for living" (Hymes, 1949, p. 35).

Playhouse teachers also strive to construct curriculum that emerges from the lives of the children. This involves continual observation and "kidwatching" or "learning about children by watching them learn" (Goodman, 1996, pp. 219-220). Kidwatchers believe that:

> … children learn language best in an environment rich with opportunities to explore interesting objects and ideas. Through observing the reading, writing, speaking, and listening of friendly interactive peers, interested kidwatching teachers can understand and support child language development (Goodman, 1996, p. 220).

Playhouse teachers are flexible and open to allowing curricular topics to emerge for inquiry, leading to multiple opportunities for talk and listening (Short, Harste, with Burke, 1996). The children engage in authentic play and discovery, which leads to the use of functional literacy practices.

Additionally, as a cooperative school, families are invited to volunteer, which creates an open dialogue and allows for the exchange of shared narratives between home and school. Playhouse parents see the school as a place for both their children and themselves to learn. As Jeanne states:

> Parents want a good safe place where they can send their children, and the parents that come here are still concerned with learning themselves: parenting skills. They're not just sending children off, they really want to be in touch with where their children are, and even though the time may be limited for them, the quality is still there.

A Socially Just Mission

Playhouse was also founded with a deep commitment to diversity of race, class, ethnicity, gender, religion, family, language, physical ability, and learning styles. As Caroline Rothschild, one of the founders, reflected: "We thought we were going to give our children a different life than we had with wars and there was going to be peace forever. We wanted the best for our children." The founding parents actively recruited families of color in 1951, a common practice for many of the cooperative schools at the time who espoused social justice commitments. And as mentioned earlier, Playhouse also established a tuition sliding scale so that families of various economic levels could have access to the school. This sliding scale is still in place today. As the *Pillars of Playhouse* (2006) mission statement states, the school hopes to:

> … arrive at a kind of global peace in a world of discord through creating a diverse community where the child's self-concept is strong. Participating in this type of community

sows the seeds for compassion, acceptance, and understanding of others. The roots of peace and the acknowledgment of others begin with the first experiences of a young child. These experiences influence a child's future beliefs about social justice (p. 3).

Diversity is embraced through the curriculum as students, teachers, and parents explore identity, cultural traditions, similarities, and differences through literature, music, nutrition, art, play, and movement.

From its inception, Playhouse acknowledged that to create a school community that welcomes diverse families regardless of race, class, or sexual orientation, it needed to devote continual attention to the ways in which families were recruited, welcomed, and integrated into the school. And no matter how deep this commitment was, to operationalize it was challenging because as Jeanne reflected:

It's hard to break through … because you find that in public places, people [are] always gravitating to the people they know where they have sameness, sameness, all the time. You find it in the lunchrooms in the schools, it always does that.

The Playhouse community was willing to work on this – but it was an ongoing challenge as you will read throughout this book.

Playhouse: The Organization of the Book

Playhouse is organized into six chapters. Each chapter is divided into four parts, beginning with an insight from Jeanne Ginsburg, followed by a personal, relatable story about my grandmother, myself or my children and our experiences at Playhouse. I then present the "pillars" of Playhouse, the core philosophy of the school, through classroom examples and interviews with Jeanne and Play-house families. These pillars include:

1. Parent Cooperative Preschool

2. Commitment to Peace, Compassion, and Acceptance

3. Beliefs about Teaching and Learning: Learning through Play and Learning as a Social Process

4. Positive Self-Concept and Positive Discipline

My intent is to provide concrete guidelines for parents to help them identify preschools that share Playhouse's philosophy, or to apply to their children's current learning experiences at school or home. I also give parents some concrete examples of what these beliefs look like in practice for early childhood educators.

More specifically, Chapter Two focuses on Playhouse's mission as a parent cooperative preschool. I explain the guiding principles, in particular the focus on relational knowing and the ethic of care that undergird the commitment to building community among children and teachers as well as among families, and then share what to look for in a preschool that values building community.

In Chapter Three, I describe the ways in which Playhouse is committed to teaching social justice and the value of a preschool that is committed to peace, compassion, and acceptance, and I then describe teaching practices that promote these values.

Chapter Four illustrates the importance of child-centered emergent curriculum and what it looks like in a preschool. The value of learning through play is presented as a means to support growth in literacy, language, problem solving, mathematics, and social interactions. I demonstrate the ways in which Playhouse teachers foster learning as a social process from a Vygotskian perspective. I discuss the ways children learn through interactions with their peers and teachers, and then I point out what social learning looks like in classrooms.

The emphasis in Chapter Five is on discussing and providing examples of how to nurture a positive self-concept in children in the preschool classroom. This chapter explores what it looks like to value the individual student and to equip them with language and tools to negotiate, compromise, and share as democratic citizens of a learning community. It also describes the ways in which positive discipline can ground children and help them become accountable for their actions.

Finally, in Chapter Six, I conclude with how Playhouse has influenced me as a parent and a socially just advocate for my children in schools.

CHAPTER 2

PLAYHOUSE: A PARENT COOPERATIVE PRESCHOOL

The two worlds of children, home and school, are reduced to one when children, parents, and teachers work collaboratively within a community of learners. This blending of worlds nurtures a partnership between home and school. Parents are involved in the school community in a variety of capacities. The work itself takes precedence over titles as we meet on common ground – a school for our children. (*Pillars of Playhouse*, 2006, p. 1)

It's hard to think of my world before Playhouse, when I wasn't a member of the Playhouse community. It has been almost 15 years since I sent my son Michael there, who is now 16. Playhouse is such a warm, loving, and welcoming environment for children and families that just draws you in, as evidenced by the fact that so many of the teachers and administrators there were once parents. Just yesterday I received an email invitation from a former Playhouse parent to attend a Playhouse reunion event. It is not surprising that we all have such fond memories of our time there. I used to find myself drawn into the community, intoxicated by the spirit, spending hours upon hours there, craving the feeling of being a part of something bigger than myself. Sheila Gallanter, a former parent and teacher from Playhouse, called it "a church" or "a synagogue" for parents with Jeanne as the spiritual leader. I laughed when she described it that way but I totally understood what she meant. I too became a disciple of Jeanne Ginsburg and Playhouse.

Playhouse and the History of Parent Cooperative Schools

> Parents hold the same broad goals for their children that teachers do. We are not competitors or opponents pulling in opposite directions. We have been strangers. We operate in different leagues. We have not talked together enough to discover all of our common understandings. Our isolation has made it hard for the teacher to be a professional, using all she knows in her classroom. It will take time to close the gap, but it can be done and the effort is worth the while. (Hymes, 1968, p. 157)

Playhouse is a parent cooperative school where all families, no matter their makeup, are welcome to be involved in their child's education. Playhouse works to foster a sense of community among children, families, and teachers based on respect for individuals and an understanding of differences. Jeanne reflects:

> Playhouse is a co-op. There is a partnership between parents and teachers working together to provide an environment that's really a healthy kind of environment for children

to be able develop at their own rate and their own style. Parents participate actively. They really administrate the school. They take charge of fee collection and the running of the school is done by the parents. Teachers, directors, and faculty work on keeping up the educational standards. We interact with each other.

Recognizing the validity of individual differences, there is no penalty for restricted parent participation, but certainly it is true that the more one is able to give in active support, the greater are the rewards. Many parents have found that the quality of their interest is more than the quantity. Not everyone is free to give large amounts of time and the school believes that only the person herself/himself is qualified to judge. Here is the strength and joy of the cooperative. Being part of Playhouse means being part of a larger family. The "open-door" policy creates a comfort level, which promotes trust between the parents, teachers, and children.

By the time Playhouse was founded in 1951, the parent cooperative movement had already garnered an extensive history. The first cooperative nursery school in the US was started in 1916 by a group of 12 faculty wives at the University of Chicago who wanted to foster "social education" for their children, "parent education" for themselves and "a little free time for Red Cross work" (Taylor, 1954, p. 3). They used space on campus and worked collaboratively with a trained teacher. After a few years, the university took over the school and it no longer remained a cooperative. From there five additional parent cooperatives arose around the country from Massachusetts to California – many affiliated with colleges like Smith or universities like UCLA. By 1950, there were a total of 285 cooperatives according to the Directory of Nursery School and Child Care Centers (Taylor, 1954).

Taylor (1954) calls parent cooperatives "a new folk movement" that exemplifies "one of the basic processes of democracy – citizen initiative to meet citizen needs" (p. 1). The key characteristic of a parent cooperative is that parents participate in the education of their young children. Taylor (1954) explains:

> Besides impacting the child's education, the greatest benefits of cooperative schools are their impact on the education of parents- mothers and father alike learn from observation and participation. These skills and insights are then utilized at home. This provides a smoother transition from school to home life. Reciprocally, having parents assist in the classroom creates a more home like environment in the school. The child has the potential to develop a strong sense of belonging in the new setting- of warmth and comfort. (pp. 5-6)

In a sense, this combats the age old problem of children as "the school's interpreters. Their answer to the old question – What did you do today? – is well known: 'Played'" (Hymes, 1968, p. 152).

To a great extent cooperatives emerged to combat the isolation that many young mothers felt as they stayed home to care for their children. They provide a social network where parents can grapple together about the challenges and celebrate the joys of parenting young children. At Playhouse, inexperienced parents and not just young mothers (as Taylor (1954) emphasizes) appreciate the realization that others experience the same feelings and anxieties. Participating in a cooperative helps parents to develop what Erickson (1951) calls their "parental sense" (p. 16). Parents and families embrace a communal space where they can learn to parent. When interviewed, Edie Weiner, a parent and social worker, recalled:

I think people felt special about Playhouse. I think the stories that people would say were, "We didn't take a course in parenting. Nobody taught us how to parent." We all had our Dr. Spock's, which was going on at the time, and Jeanne. That's who we consulted … We learned at Jeanne's as much as we learned at our parents … I learned so much at Playhouse – not only about parenting but about myself … I grew at Playhouse as a person. I really did. So it was very important for me.

In some ways, the families benefitted as much if not more than the children from Playhouse. They were invited to be vulnerable, to work on themselves as parents, and to make lifelong friendships. Edie Weiner continues:

I think those of us who were involved probably did get more out of the school as parents. I think the children did regardless. I would not give up those years for anything. They were wonderful years for me. My friends today are people, many of them I made friends with at Playhouse. It's a time in your life … I guess I'm going to say something personal. My husband passed away five years ago and so friendships change and you make new friends. I was saying to somebody, one of my old friends, "but it's not the same." They become friends but they don't share your history. The friends that I've had from Playhouse know my history. They knew my children when they were little. You can talk about those kinds of things with them. I think at that time in your life when you have young children, it is a time that you are looking for friendship. Your college friends have gone different ways and some of us have left the workforce … or they're not having children. You know, you're at different stages. These people are all at the same stage of life as you are.

By being a part of a community, rather than simply sending their children to a school, families feel they have opportunities to contribute but also are invited to be vulnerable and work on their parenting skills. This rings true throughout another parent, Ronnie Stern's narrative when during her interview with me she recalls her first days at Playhouse in 1969:

> So I thought where could I send my kids and I remembered Playhouse ... I walk in the door with my eldest son, and actually I was pregnant with my third who was going to be born in November that school year, and I was like totally overwhelmed. I walked in. I have these two little babies and another one on the way. Doreen was teacher there. She was a new teacher. And she put her arms around me, and she said, "I want you to just sit down right here." She first looked at me, gave me a more loving reading than my own mother. It was like, here is a home. It was a home. At that time we came every week, once a week. My day was Friday. I still remember coming once a week and cooping, and it was like I discovered America. I loved it, it fed me, it fed them, I stayed, I taught there, I taught the little 2 year old class, what did they call it, presidents of the board thing, I did that for two years, but for me the kernel of it is what happened with the adults. The seed was planted with the adults, who carried it in their homes. My memories are about staff training ... parent groups with Jeanne, relationships with other women ... I carried that my life, with my life. That was my therapy. It was everything. So those are the memories that I have.

Building a Parent Cooperative Community

Playhouse works to foster a sense of community among children, families, and staff. Our community is constructed based on respect for individuals and an understanding of their differences. Being part of a learning community helps to extend the concept of being part of a family, lays the foundation for the construction of future relationships, and recognizes the role of others as a life support system. Several explicit methods are used to build community at Playhouse. At the beginning of the school year, families and children receive welcome letters from their teachers and are asked to fill out interest surveys so that teachers can become better acquainted with children and their families – including a question that asks what is your child's favorite book as well as what special skills do you have as a parent that you may want to share with the community.

Recognizing how important it is for families to feel welcome and to begin to understand the Playhouse way, the Board very deliberately plans the first weeks of school. In particular, they create a staggered opening day schedule where different classes begin on different days, so that they can devote time to each and every new child and family. In order to create the smoothest separation for the child and family, specific attention is paid to the ways in which children transition into the classroom. This is in sharp contrast to the traditional ways that children enter schools, where their parents are often asked to leave them at the door, not enter the school building or the classroom, and separate in a clean and sometimes sharp fashion. Instead, at Playhouse there is intentional attention paid to developing trusting relations between parents, teachers, and children. As Hymes (1968) writes:

We have to build good personal relationships with parents. Mothers and fathers must know their child's teacher, you must know the parents. Strangers cannot communicate. Strangers seldom feel trust and confidence. Distance does not lend enchantment, it only breeds suspicion (p. 153).

Playhouse purposely staggers the start date of different classes, so that more attention can be paid to each child and family. In this way, during the first few weeks of school:

> … parents and teachers get a chance to get to know one another. Individual children often need their parents with them for the beginning days or longer … parents need comfort too … More and more teachers find it easy to say the more decent words: "Stay! Stay as long as your child needs you … I am glad to have you here." And these teachers are glad. The parent has the chance to see a good program in operation. The teacher and the parent have time some time to talk. (Hymes, 1968, p. 154)

Realizing how important this was to her for her own children, Edie Weiner describes the ways in which Playhouse uniquely approached her child's first encounters at Playhouse in contrast to other preschools:

> I remember when I was looking with my first child for schools. At that point, there was a year long waiting list to get into Playhouse. So I started looking a year before – we weren't even living in the area. I had gone to some of the temple pre-schools and stuff and my son and I were very attached. He clung to my side and I looked at them and the usual kinds of things were going on and then we came to Playhouse and nobody asked him, pushed him to come

over, sit down, join us ... they allowed him to stay. I was observing the classroom. It was Jessie Hurdoch's. She left before I became a parent here. I was watching her read a story to the children. The children had come over in a circle. David was by my side. And some of the children didn't want to come so she read to the children who were in that circle and she kept referencing children that were at the other side of the room, including them in the story without them having to do something they didn't want to do. I thought that's beautiful. I really like that. Then I was in Jeanne's room and she let us be and then she asked one of the children if they wanted to come over and ask David to paint. She didn't do it and it was so beautiful. My son left my side and came over to this little board. I still have that little board, in a little treasure box – my favorite thing. That was his first pre-school experience. It wasn't a forced thing. It was just this kind of thing that was gradual.

Welcoming Breakfasts

Additionally, the Board hosts welcome breakfasts with coffee, juice, bagels, and fruit which give families a space to transition into the pre-school experience. And as in any community whether in the classroom or the neighborhood, established members take responsibility to welcome and orient new families. At Playhouse much of the work focuses on veteran or experienced Playhouse families helping new people through the separation process from their children, as the moms and dads are just as anxious if not more anxious than their children. The breakfasts serve as a way for them to be reassured, consoled, and welcomed into a safe space where they can feel vulnerable. These social events also give new families an opportunity to get to know members of the Playhouse community.

I remember our first few weeks at Playhouse with Michael, who began at the age of two years and 5 months old. Those first breakfasts reminded me of why Playhouse felt like such a perfect fit. I quickly realized that I was not just sending my child to a new school, but that I was becoming part of a nurturing community of other families with similar interests, concerns, and even politics to a great extent. I immediately felt like I wasn't alone. This yearly event so clearly represents the principles of Playhouse and the foresight and knowledge that the founders had about the necessity to build a safe and trusting community for the families as well as the children.

In many ways, Playhouse nurtures families through their early years of parenting. Those breakfasts set a precedent for my future interactions at Playhouse. I would often find myself lingering after drop off either chatting with the other mothers in Maria's class, the hallway, or the library. Sometimes I would end up in the office chatting with Anat, Jeanne, or Marybeth. And then when I served as the co-president for several years, I was involved in organizing the breakfasts and welcoming other parents into the fold. Remarkably, even today I still find myself lingering even eight years later, when I do not have children there.

Parent Orientation Meeting

Besides the welcome breakfasts, at the beginning of the year, Playhouse organizes a parent orientation meeting where the teachers, directors, and the Board introduce themselves and share the mission of the school. Later parents are invited to meet with their child's teacher in the classroom. My first parent orientation was probably the most memorable, especially because I walked into it unsure of what it would be like. As we entered the school, we were greeted and asked to fill out a name tag, grab a Playhouse directory, and some refreshments. The Playhouse directory contained all of the contact information for each child separated into individual classes – another way that the Playhouse Board attempted to build community both inside and outside of the school. Tables were lined in the hallway filled with healthy snacks and goodies, many baked by the families, for the orientation.

We arrived to a classroom filled with people sitting on folding chairs and on the floor. Most of the classroom furniture had been removed except for the borders lined with bookshelves, shelves of blocks, cars, and toys. I remember being amazed by the diversity of the people – young, old, white, Latino, African American, Indian, Asian, in couples, mothers together, fathers together, some adolescent siblings, grandparents, all people present because of their connection to a young Playhouse child. Family members had come from work in suits or blue jeans, some having left their other children with a babysitter, all anxious to hear about Playhouse and feel either welcomed to the Playhouse community or renew their commitment to the place. As we got situated, I found a small space on the floor, and we looked to the front of the room where the directors and teachers sat. There were family members packed into this small space and spilling out into the hallway.

The orientation began with some introductions from the directors, teachers, and parent Board. Then members of the audience were invited to share how they came to Playhouse. The stories were touching and heartwarming. One woman said that she was a Playhouse grandmother and that her older grandchildren had attended Playhouse and now she was back with their much younger siblings.

Many talked about hearing about Playhouse through friends, neighbors, and on the playground (that free network that seems to be the perfect vehicle to spread the word about Playhouse) and just as I felt, many shared that they knew Playhouse was the perfect fit for their family the minute they came here. These stories set the warm tone and environment for the rest of the session.

As if that wasn't endearing and reassuring enough, they then moved to the Jeanne segment of the presentation. Now up until that moment I had met Jeanne and had seen her in passing, but I had yet to really connect with her. I do not think I could have anticipated at that moment how important a role she would play in my life. They began by showing a short film of Jeanne talking about her beliefs and the philosophy of Playhouse. While flashing images of Jeanne and children at Playhouse, the narrator began:

> If you are a dreamer, come in. If you are a dreamer, a wisher, a liar, a hoper, a prayer, a magic bean buyer, if you are a pretender, come. Sit by my fire, for we have some flax golden tales to spin. Come in. Come in.

I was mesmerized by Jeanne in the film – it was as if she were speaking directly to me. Her voice and her tone were so calming and inviting. She spoke to parents about what they might want from a preschool:

> Parents want a good safe place where they can send their children, and the parents that come here are still concerned with learning themselves: parenting skills. They're not just sending children off, they really want to be in touch with where their children are, and even though the time may be limited for them, the quality is still there.

Her words began to ease my insecurity and stress about parenting. Playhouse would become a place where I too would benefit, where we would learn to be good parents, and where my children would thrive.

School/Family Events

Continuing to extend that subtle yet inviting welcome to the families, during the school year a family/teacher directory is issued and a biweekly memo is sent out via e-mail, sharing highlights from each classroom written by teachers. Additionally there are several social family events that are organized on weekends throughout the school year to encourage a sense of community. Some of these include pot luck family picnics at the school at the beginning and end of the school year when families, teachers, and children can socialize and make connections. In the winter, the Board hosts a series of parental educational workshops on topics that have been suggested by the families. These are held on weekends at the school and provide a forum for parents to question, reflect, and gather information around a particular topic. Finally, for a very long time, fireside chats with Jeanne were offered as another way to encourage parental enrichment. In general, these very concrete strategies remind families that they can approach the Board, administrators, and teachers at any time.

Parent Volunteering

Parents are welcomed and invited to become active participants of the learning community. A sense of belonging and being accepted helps parents to support the educational process of their children. Playhouse's "open-door" policy creates a comfort level which promotes trust between the parents, teachers, and children. Parents have access to teachers and administrators both during school hours as well as after school hours – staff phone numbers are included in the student directory. In addition, community is fostered through the varied ways that parents are involved in the school.

As part of the agreement to be a member of a cooperative school, parents are expected to volunteer their time however and whenever they can. Edie Weiner remembered that this was about parents doing what they were comfortable doing:

> I remember saying to Jeanne, "The same parents are volunteering. You know … not everybody's involved." I remember Jeanne saying to me, "There are parents who can, parents who can't and parents who won't and you need to accept that about them."

For some families this entails volunteering in the classrooms, but for others it may mean being a class parent, helping with building maintenance, grocery shopping, caring for animals, kitchen cleaning, gardening, or organizing the library. In fact, once a season, families are invited to spend a Saturday morning working on the upkeep of the school, whether that involves painting, cleaning, building shelving, or any other tasks necessary for the school. The general attitude at Playhouse is that all families have something to offer the community and volunteering is not a one size fits all model.

For families whose children are in the cooperative classrooms, parents volunteer regularly as teaching assistants. In other classes, parents are invited to volunteer when they are able to. The ways in which parents assist in their child's classroom are developed in collaboration with the teachers through sharing culture, traditions, food, music, and stories in the classroom. Much like Moll, Amanti, Neff, and Gonzalez's (1992) concept of "funds of knowledge," these invitations provide opportunities for children to recognize that their home traditions are important in school.

For example, Playhouse uses holidays as an opportunity for parents to share their family traditions and for children to learn about one another. Families are invited to come into the classroom and share their traditions in multiple forms including songs, cooking, games, picture books, and art. When asked to reflect on how family holidays are included at Playhouse, Danielle, one of the all day school teachers, shares her perspective on parents volunteering in the classroom around the holidays:

> Eliminating holidays as the basis for curriculum planning does not mean ignoring them altogether. Instead, at Playhouse, we incorporate these special times into a larger concept such as a shared celebration or family tradition. The celebration tends to be shared in a low key manner from an eclectic, cultural point of view usually incorporating songs, stories, and foods. We encourage families to share something from the holidays that are celebrated in the home. Last year for example, we had the pleasure of tasting Haroset, touched an oil lamp from Diwali, examined clothing from Ethiopia, investigated various Chinese yo-yos, and explored and compared home rituals associated with Christmas, Hanukkah, and Kwanza through various in depth discussions pertaining to "families" and "homes." The children automatically make connections with their own lives. We need to also keep in mind that holiday rituals/traditions need not be confined only to specific time frames. They can be observed weekly/monthly through storytelling, finger plays, songs, props, or healthy foods.

When my children Michael and Griffin were at Playhouse, they learned about many different cultural traditions from their friends' families, and they shared some of their own traditions too. In Griffin's second year at Playhouse, he had a classmate named Sara who was adopted from China. Around Chinese New Year, her mother shared an explanation of the holiday through making paper Chinese lanterns with the children, sharing some Mandarin phrases to say Happy New Year and eating fortune cookies. Griffin got a meaningful introduction to Chinese New Year through the eyes of his friend.

I also volunteered in Michael's class. Because we are an interfaith family that celebrates both Hanukkah and Christmas, we were able to share our traditions from two holidays. Michael appreciated that several of his friends celebrated more than one holiday like he did. For Hanukkah, I made latkes with the children, read *My First Cha-nukah* (De Paola, 1986), played the dreidel game with small groups of children, and lit the candles of Michael's personal menorah. At Christmas time, my sisters and I made gingerbread cookies with the children, an activity that we do every year together at home. We talked about how we also decorate our tree with lights to celebrate. We read *Light the Lights: A Story about Celebrating Hanukkah & Christmas* (Moorman, 1994), a book that highlights how lights are common across Hanukkah and Christmas. A few days later, another parent and one of the assistant teachers introduced some of the values of Kwanza and lit candles. Michael so embraced the three holidays and their similarities that he decided to declare them all his own.

Besides helping the teacher, these are opportunities for parents to observe their children in action and engage with them in very different ways than they do at home. Taylor (1967) clarifies the importance of cooperative schools for parents when she writes:

> The unique value of the learning provided by cooperatives
> is what parents carry back into guiding and living with their
> children at home, since in a very real sense they are their
> children's most constant and important teachers. (p. 144)

Building Community Within the Classroom

The Playhouse curriculum furthers a vision of community through a focus on child-centered learning and a commitment to reciprocal relationships between teachers and children. The classrooms become a learning environment that promotes awareness of the needs of others and the larger community. To do this, Playhouse first begins with helping children to develop a positive self-concept and an appreciation for their uniqueness and individual differences. These relationships are nurtured through calling teachers by their first names, sharing meals together, exchanging personal stories, listening to children, participating in class meetings, modeling conflict resolution and compassion, and using positive discipline on both an individual and developmental level where we attempt to resolve conflict instead of punishing.

Through play and discussion with the teachers, children are encouraged to express their needs. At Playhouse, children are heard, seen, and understood, rather than seen and not heard. Children are invited to be self-reflective, to understand and accept themselves, and to be able to verbalize their feelings. They are guided to discover personal strategies for comforting themselves and dealing with feelings like anger, frustration, and disappointment, so that they can successfully self-regulate their emotions and behaviors. Safe spaces are created to talk about difficult issues, think critically, allow children to take a stand, and take risks while learning. Teachers encourage children to have second choices so that they do not feel stuck.

In particular, teachers nurture the self-confidence of children to develop by:

- Accepting children for who they are.

- Welcoming children in the morning.

- Using positive language.

- Gauging students' feelings.

- Empowering children with respect for their personal interests.

- Taking an interest in an individual's work and play.

- Encouraging children to share meaningful stories and items from home.

- Asking children to think about the people that they want to be.

- Teachers also connect with children by:

- Sharing personal experiences to humanize adults.

- Making comments that indicate a shared feeling such as "I love that story too".

- Praising students.

- Providing children with empowering opportunities through choice.

- Inviting children to have opinions.

- Having appropriate expectations for the children.

- Instilling a sense of individual responsibility.

- Allowing children to struggle.

- Developing self-help skills such as pouring juice, cleaning up, putting on coats and shoes, and washing hands.

Playhouse teachers are selected not only for their educational degrees and certifications, but also for the dispositions that they possess and the ways in which they are able to become members of the Playhouse community. They teach from a humanistic approach, drawing from their own lived experiences and instincts when they interact and respond to the children. The teachers are unique because they possess dispositions of openness, caring, and reflectiveness. They prioritize listening to the children rather than talking at them. The Playhouse environment fosters collaboration among teachers rather than competition. Teachers are encouraged to recognize one another's strengths.

More specifically, Playhouse teachers are passionate about their roles in the lives of the young children in their classrooms. They have a sense of self-acceptance in order to instill a positive self-image in their children. They demonstrate social behaviors that help our children to think about ways to interact with one another. They are flexible and understand that there is no right way of approaching an idea. They encourage students to talk as a means to gain an understanding of each other's perspectives, and they value and promote various questions and perspectives from the children. They provide students with praise as an encouragement to go on rather than as a stop sign.

Teachers listen to and work with the children, parents, and the Playhouse community. In particular, they work collaboratively with parents to address the needs of the child. They strive to develop positive relationships with children by playing, eating, and cleaning up with them. They also engage with students through reading, sharing stories, talking, and listening. They create a more equitable atmosphere by using everyone's first name, physically getting down to the children's level, and interacting with them in peaceful, nonconfrontational, and respectful ways. Because all of the classes have multiple teachers, successful teamwork and collaboration are modeled for the children.

There is also a sense of community among staff, the directors, and the Playhouse Board. Teachers are greatly respected as professionals and experts in their field. They are trusted and have ownership of their teaching. They expect that the teachers are reflective practitioners, always taking time to think about their interactions and practices. This is fostered through sharing knowledge and experiences at weekly staff meetings, participating in staff development together, sharing spaces and resources between classes, being recognized by a yearly teacher appreciation luncheon, participating in school wide activities, and meeting for school gatherings.

Cooperative School Governance

The Playhouse School Board, which is the governing committee, is made up of current parents. The officers of the cooperative are President(s), Vice-President(s), Treasurer, Secretary, and Accounts Payable. They are elected by the general membership and serve from July through June of the following year. The current officers and often the immediate past presidents constitute the Board of Trustees. Special committees are set up for individual functions as needed. The duties of the officers and the Board are explicitly stated in the By-Laws. The Co-President(s) lead the Board meetings and organize Board members into committees to facilitate the activities of the school. Some of the committees include finance, fund raising, publicity, educational workshops, and family events. The Board also appoints the Directors, adopts the yearly budget, and sets teachers' salaries. Board meetings are held once a month and are always open. Any member may attend and have a voice.

The Business Director and the Educational Director collaboratively manage the daily running of the school. The responsibilities of the Business Director include but are not limited to finance, facility maintenance, registration, and licensing. The responsibilities of the Educational Director include but are not limited to curriculum development, teacher supervision and mentoring, educational materials, parent liaison, professional development for teachers, and assessing and fulfilling children's needs.

The long-term advisory committee is made up of former parents. This is a formal way for alumni to stay connected to Playhouse and help to maintain the "Playhouse way." This committee counsels the board in a manner consistent with the educational philosophy and practice of the founders of Playhouse. The Committee provides input to the Board on educational policy, long-term planning, location of Playhouse, major capital expenditures, and additional matters indicated by the Board. The membership and terms served on this committee are stated explicitly in the By-Laws. This connection with the past perpetuates a sense of history and continuous commitment to the clear vision and philosophies of Jeanne Ginsberg, the founding families of Playhouse, and subsequent families through the years.

This chapter, although focused on the strategies and operations of Playhouse, serves an important role in the book as it demonstrates in very concrete ways how to put into practice the foundational beliefs about the value and significance of family and school connections. Too often schools claim to be spaces where families are invited, and yet there are very few authentic and flexible opportunities for families to become involved. Playhouse uniquely has developed a wide variety of means by which parents can be active members of the school community, not only through both volunteering time and energy but also through social interactions as citizens.

CHAPTER 3

TWO BOYS IN LOVE: A COMMITMENT TO PEACE, COMPASSION, AND ACCEPTANCE

Luckily for those who despair of society's ever being made into a kinder place, young children are far more empathetic by nature than we are prone to believe. They are enormously interested in being in the company of other children and are persistently curious about those we seem different. By the time children enter preschool, they are experienced people-watchers, and they know what makes someone laugh or cry. (Paley, 1997)

I was drawn to Playhouse before I had even visited the school because it helped me to reconcile an internal conflict that I faced about where I would be happy to live and raise my children. I grew up mostly in New York City, and spent a good portion of my childhood and adolescence abroad. My dad was a banker and we lived in Paris, Sevenoaks, Athens, and Manama from the time I was eight to twelve, and thereafter I spent my summers in France, Spain, Italy, and Japan. In my early twenties, I lived and worked as an urban middle school teacher in NYC. After these experiences, I had a really hard time agreeing to live in suburban New Jersey. The problem was that Mark, my husband, had never lived in the city before, and when we first made the move back East, he could not get his head around urban life. It is funny that seventeen years later he thinks he could make the move and now I am unsure!

What was the main issue for me then? I wanted to live among diversity, the way I had while I was growing up. I wanted my children to have friends of all races, classes, ethnicities, and languages, and I wanted them to see that a family could mean many different things. Now, much to the contradiction of my old assumptions, there are communities in suburban New Jersey that are diverse, such as Montclair, Maplewood, and West Orange. Unfortunately, when it came time to buy a house, we couldn't find anything in those towns that we could afford. So we ended up in Verona, which borders Montclair and West Orange. Verona is a lovely little idyllic town – the children walk to school on their own, and there are crossing guards, block parties, a pool, town sports, and a beautiful park designed by Olmsted, the creator of Central Park – but it has little diversity. Many of the Verona families are just like us, New Yorkers who escaped the struggles of New York life, but just as many are Verona born and raised.

With such a lack of diversity, I felt even more compelled to find a preschool that was committed to creating a school community made of families from different backgrounds. And so, as I mentioned, I was really in love with Playhouse simply from its description. This principle was also aligned with my beliefs at work in the more general field of teacher education. I wanted to walk my talk instead of simply talking the talk. I wanted my children to develop a worldview of acceptance and openness to difference, and Playhouse seemed the perfect place to build that foundation. I had a hunch that learning alongside children whose families encompassed many races, classes, languages, abilities, religions, and sexual orientations would influence Michael and Griffin, but I had no idea how deep their social justice roots would grow.

Two Boys Can Love Each Other

Michael entered kindergarten at our local Verona school after he completed three years at Playhouse. Although he never expressed it and maybe never even realized it, I can imagine it was quite a shock to go from a classroom that was so diverse to one that felt almost homogeneous. One day, he invited two of his friends, Olivia and Kyle, over for lunch and a play date. Olivia and Michael have grown up together and are almost like siblings. Olivia's mom, Laura, is one of my best friends and brought us to Verona and our street of Morningside Road. At the time, Kyle was a newer friend.

After I prepared the usual Kraft macaroni and cheese and gave them their Hershey chocolate milks, I left the kitchen to give them some privacy and sat at the dining room table in the room adjacent. I was in the perfect spot to eavesdrop on their oh-so-honest conversation. The kids started to talk about the children in their classes and whom they liked and loved. They began to go through a list:

Olivia: Well, what about Brendan M.?

Michael: Well, I like him as a friend.

Kyle: Yeah. He is really smart.

Olivia: What about Olivia W.? Do you like her as more than a friend, Michael?

Michael: (giggle, giggle) No. She's, she's just a friend.

(I knew he had a little crush on her.)

Kyle: I don't really know her.

Olivia: I think she likes David as more than a friend.

Kyle: And Lucas?

Olivia: He's okay. I don't see him at school much. Michael, you just like him as a friend, right?

Michael: Yeah, he's just a friend. But you know, two boys can love each other. It doesn't have to be a boy and a girl.

(Okay, that really peaked my interest. I couldn't wait to hear how Michael was going to explain this.)

Michael: You know, you can have all different kinds of families. Two boys can love each other, two girls can love each other, or a boy and a girl can love each other.

Olivia: Yeah. I know.

Kyle: Really? But how do two boys or two girls have babies? I thought you needed a mom and a dad.

(At this point, Michael used his expert voice. Michael always sounds like he is an expert on every topic – he puts on an almost scholarly tone. I wonder where he got that from?)

Michael: That's easy. If a family has two dads or two moms, then they can adopt a baby. It's no big deal. One of my friends at Playhouse has two moms.

Olivia: Yeah. It's really no biggie.

In that moment, I felt a mixture of great joy, pride, and anxiety. I was so proud of Michael as he matter-of-factly stated that essentially he was an advocate for same-sex families, but I was also nervous about the possible repercussions in my not-so-liberal town of Verona. I knew that Ollie's mom would get a chuckle from the conversation, but I did not really know Kyle's family. Needless to say, in this instance, there were no consequences. Of course since then, I have heard my adult neighbors and sometimes their children make numerous prejudiced statements about race, religion, gender, and sexual orientation. Sometimes I realize just how much I have raised my children to be independent thinkers.

Michael and I had never really had a direct conversation about the makeup of different families, but clearly it was something that he had thought a bit about. Later, when he was alone, I asked him quietly if he had ever talked about this at Playhouse in Maria's class, but his memory seemed to be foggy. At the end of elementary school when I first talked to him about this conversation, hoping for some insight, I got none. The only thing he told me with quiet emotion was that it bothered him when people used the word "gay" as an insult. Two years ago, as a freshman, over nine years after this conversation, Michael quietly took an activist stand and joined the Gay/Straight Alliance. When I asked him why (he is not the sort of kid who every wants to stick out or be noticed), he said, "In solidarity Mom. Isn't that what you raised me to do? Isn't it about social justice?"

When two of his classmates with whom he had gone through middle school came out as transgendered two years ago as freshmen, Michael's social justice stance kept him grounded, open-minded, and supportive of his friends. When I asked prodding questions to get a sense of the school community's acceptance, he got defensive and said "Mommmmm! It is not a big deal. Why are you asking me so many questions?" This may seem trivial to some but to me it reminds me of the significance of developing a strong foundation around acceptance, compassion, and tolerance early on. Not all of the students at Michael's school feel or act the way he does, although I try to remain hopeful that issues of gender and sexual identities are rapidly changing in the United States.

This shy expression of protest warms my heart, especially because of the continuous presence of bullying, harassment, murder, and hatred of the queer community both within our own local Verona schools as well as more generally in U.S. society. Although I know from much of the research that young gay and bisexual men under the age of 26 are at a significantly greater risk of suicide or self-harm because of homophobic discriminatory and marginal-ized acts (London School of Hygiene and Tropical Medicine, 2016). I don't have to look beyond my own community to realize that harassment and bullying torment the lives of our youth. Just this past August we were saddened to hear that a young Verona man who was supposed to enter 9th grade took his life. He had suffered horrible bullying in middle school and had been removed from school and home schooled for a year and a half. We believe that the anxiety of meeting with the high school principal and potentially subjecting himself to harassment because of his sexual identity led to his suicide. I know that this young man echoes the stories of people like Asher Brown (thirteen years old), Billy Lucas (fifteen years old), Justin Aaberg (fifteen years old), Seth Walsh (thirteen years old), and Tyler Clementi at Rutgers University in New Jersey.

Nationally, we spent late June, 2016 grieving the 50 lives that were lost from the mass shooting at Pulse, the LGBT dance club in downtown Orlando, Florida. This tragic event, one of the most deadly mass shootings in the US to date, is particularly troubling because places like Pulse are important spaces where people can both feel free to be themselves but also where they seek community and safety. How strange to imagine that this happened during Pride month, a time when we recognize and celebrate the LGBT community and their civil rights. Devastated by this brutal display of hatred, we are reminded of the urgency of educating young children to open their hearts and minds to others and understand what it means to "be in someone else's shoes." As Lin Manuel Miranda, in his acceptance speech on June 12, 2016 for the Tony for *Hamilton* stated:

> When senseless acts of tragedy remind us that nothing here is promised, not one day. This show is proof that history remembers we live through times when hate and fear seem stronger. We rise and fall and light from dying embers remembrances that hope and love last longer. Love is love is love is love is love is love is love is love cannot be killed or swept aside … Now fill the world with music, and love, and pride.

I only hope that Michael will continue to feel strongly about his convictions and will advocate for others who are being ostracized.

Can I solely attribute this socially just stance to Playhouse? Probably not entirely, but I do believe that those early years lay the foundation for a child's future worldview, and that having the experience of going to school with children of such diverse backgrounds as well as being in a school community that values acceptance and compassion opens a child to the world. In the teacher preparation courses that I teach at MSU, I often notice that students who grew up in middle class, white, homogeneous settings tend to be the most apprehensive about working in urban classrooms. Just spending some time in a place like Newark helps them to feel more comfortable. There is something fearful about the unknown. Playhouse created a space for Michael and Griffin that helped them to build their known and create a strong awareness of the value of respecting and accepting all people.

Commitment to Peace, Compassion, and Acceptance

Playhouse was founded in 1951, with a deep commitment to diversity of race, class, ethnicity, gender, religion, family, language, physical ability, and learning styles. Although the founders were predominantly Jewish and middle class, in the aftermath of World War II, they were especially focused on providing a learning community for themselves and their families that embraced all people and promoted peace. They did not want to segregate themselves and send their children to Jewish preschools. They wanted a school where their children could learn to be open, compassionate, caring, and accepting in practice, not just in theory. Caroline Rothschild, one of the founding parents, helped to illustrate this when she explained their ideals for the school: "We found all kinds of people and our aim was to have it mixed. We would have done anything for a black person. And it ended up that we had Ed Bowser. He had come on his own and he was brilliant. We were idealistic and liberal" (Ed Bowser was an African American architect from Orange). They hoped that as adults, their children would become peace advocates who were comfortable in their own shoes as well as the shoes of others.

But wanting to create a school community that was socially just needed more than simply recruiting families of color. That was only the first step. As Enid Lee reflects in an interview with *Rethinking Schools* (1995): "I have met some teachers who think that just because they have kids from different races and backgrounds, they have a multicultural classroom. Bodies of kids are not enough" (p. 10). The Playhouse founders also had to think about the instructional and operational practices that the school used in order to create a learning community that promoted acceptance and compassion.

Developing a socially just instructional stance in a preschool can be daunting, especially if the founders and Jeanne were intentionally hoping not to provide just a surface experience for the children and their families. They did not want to simply symbolically include the voices of others through food or a particular cultural practice. Nor did they want to create isolated instances of multicultural learning by including for example a special unit on Native Americans. Too often early childhood educators and parents too shy away from having more in-depth discussions with their children about culture. But as Derman-Sparks (1995) writes:

> Culture is not an abstraction to young children. It is lived and learned every day through the way family members interact, through language, family stories, family values, and spiritual life, through household customs and the work family members do, and through society's values as transmitted by television and children's books (p. 17).

Unfortunately, too often programs and teachers reinforce misinformation and stereotypes even if that is not their intentions. The founders were aware of this and instead hoped that Playhouse's emergent curriculum would reflect the values of caring and social change and would encourage the children to think critically about the world in which they lived and talk back to it. Their circle time could be safe spaces to show support for one another but also question and disrupt the norms of society and imagine a community that accepts others. They aspired to foster a space where all children and teachers were valued and could speak freely, listen actively, dream, invent, and imagine. Ayers (2004) echoes this concept when he writes: "A good school is an intimate community where children find unconditional acceptance" (p. 41). This involves teachers both creating caring relationships with their students and families but also helping students to "develop the capacity to care" through dialogue, listening, and supportive language (Noddings, 1992, p. 18).

This sort of an environment has the potential to provide children with the seeds of what it means to be a democratic citizen who belongs to a community, has responsibility to that community, but also can contribute individualized perspectives. This is a difficult utopian vision for schools – one that necessitates continually tending – but one that has enormous potential to impact children and the ways in which they view their own possibilities in the world. Playhouse would become a place where together teachers and students could explore notions of gender, family, race, environment, language, sexuality, and economic class. They could discuss hurtful words and name-calling and consider other ways to interact with one another. They could make sense of tragedy in the world – no matter how small like the death of a ladybug, or how great like some of the current tragedies in the news. Classrooms committed to social justice also invite students to engage in critical literacy and problematize objects or narratives that are taken for granted in their daily lives like particular toys, stories, ways that we speak to one another, current events, products we consume like juice boxes (Vazquez, 2004), or really any text or image. To put these into practice, some of the questions that they asked themselves included:

> What kinds of pictures are up on the wall? What kinds of festivals are celebrated? What are the rules and expectations in the classroom in terms of what languages are acceptable? What kinds of interactions are encouraged? How are the kids grouped? (Lee in *Rethinking Schools* (1995), p. 10)

Sliding Scale Tuition

Playhouse was conceptualized as a cooperative, non-sectarian, nonprofit preschool, which strives to invite traditional and non-traditional families into their learning community. Many of the school's administrative decisions attempt to fulfill this deeply held principle. Each year great care is taken through the admissions and hiring processes to ensure that the students and teachers of the school are diverse. From the inception of the school, Jeanne and the founding parents implemented a sliding scale tuition system, in which families pay tuition based on their total family income for the year. They believed that the cost of tuition should not impede membership into the Playhouse community. In an interview, Carol Marcus, a parent from the 1970s, reflected on the benefit of economic diversity:

> It was a very important thing. And the kids, because they all slept at each other's houses and had play dates, didn't care. It didn't mean anything to them and their parents didn't impose on them. You know, they didn't say, "Oh, they are rich or they're poor or they live over there in that neighborhood."

A partial scholarship program, supported by some small grants and donations, was also developed to support the needs of different families. Additionally, since the late 1990s, Playhouse has been located in downtown West Orange, providing access to families that live in the local community.

Supporting Diverse Needs of Families

Playhouse also paid close attention to the needs of its diverse families. Up until the early 1970s, they only offered half-day cooperative classes. This was really fashioned for families where at least one parent stayed at home, something that was becoming a privilege for some, rather than a norm. With women going to work, families needed full-time care for their children, and therefore Playhouse instituted an all-day school option for those who needed it, which is still in place today as there are three all-day school classrooms. Although parents in the all-day school classes cannot volunteer in the classroom on a regular basis, they are still invited to become involved in the school in any way that makes sense to them. This is another administrative decision that helps to support diversity at Playhouse. Families are welcomed to contribute to the school in their own ways, rather than conforming to one mode.

Diverse Recruitment

Even with these systems in place, recruiting diverse families has always been a challenge for Playhouse. Every year that I served on the Parent Board, this was an issue of discussion, and it continues to be now that I serve on the Advisory Board. Interestingly, Playhouse's most effective recruitment strategy has always been through word of mouth. When one family of color feels comfortable as a member of the Playhouse community, then others usually follow. This necessitates asking families of color to help recruit other families. This strategy can sometimes be difficult to navigate. You never want a family to feel like they represent a whole community, but Playhouse fosters an environment where people engage, even if the conversations are uncomfortable.

Addressing Diversity Through the Curriculum

Besides administratively, diversity is welcomed through the curriculum, as students, teachers, and parents explore identity, cultural traditions, similarities, and differences through literature, music, nutrition, art, play, and movement. This can manifest in a variety of ways, including the books shared with the children, the presentations of cultural and religious traditions, the representations of children and families, and beginning conversations about difference, individualism, acceptance, and peace. For example, when I was a Playhouse parent, I appreciated that in December the children were exposed to many cultural traditions, rather than simply Christmas. Michael felt comforted that there were many children in his class who celebrated multiple holidays like Hanukkah, Christmas, and Kwanzaa. He enjoyed investigating the parallel ways that light is used in the three unique cultural celebrations. The children appreciate comparing and contrasting these traditions, looking for commonalities as well as differences. These classroom practices are supported by frequent professional development, an extensive library of children's books that address issues of difference, as well as an openness at staff meetings to discuss the challenges that these issues raise.

At Playhouse, there is a commitment to nurturing children's life-long development of peaceful advocacy and compassion for others. Their experiences at Playhouse lay the foundation for their roles in society as leaders, responsible followers, moral beings and citizens. The first step to accepting others and creating a peaceful environment is to accept oneself and develop inner peace. Playhouse teachers create a true learning community where children develop positive attitudes of belonging, valuing all members, sharing, communicating feelings and viewpoints, and listening to others and accepting other perspectives. They encourage children to strive to live harmoniously through modeling respect, teaching democratically, using positive discipline, and nurturing conflict resolution. They create opportunities for students to explore the ways in which language has power. One cornerstone of the curriculum is social and language based, and therefore there are multiple opportunities to discuss and share feelings and ideas. During circle time and throughout the day, questions such as "How do you feel today?", "What did we do today?", "What did you do today to make yourself feel better?", and "What did you do to make someone else feel better?" are discussed.

Children are encouraged not to judge others but to learn to value everyone for their uniqueness and individuality. A small example of this is a more recent story that Edie Wiener, a former parent and teacher at Playhouse, and more recently a hired social worker consultant, shared about bringing her granddaughter to visit Playhouse. While they were spending time with Jeanne, she took them in to look at the Madagascar hissing cockroaches. Edie shared this:

> My granddaughter is one of these little princess people and she pulled away. I said, "They are kind of scary." Jeanne said, "They're different." Scary was giving it a value judgment. And Jeanne took the value … and the magic was still there. That's Jeanne. She took the value judgment away from it and said, "They are different. Let's take a look at them."

Playhouse teachers model ways to observe differences without placing judgment. This stance also applies to approaching children of different cultures, religions, families, and children with disabilities. Edie Weiner recalls the story of Jason, a blind child, who was enrolled at Playhouse in the 1970s. The inclusion of children with disabilities has become a relatively common practice in schools since the IDEA act of 1994, but it was unheard of in the 1970s. Edie shares:

> His name was Jason and he was blind. I remember the parent in that class who said, "Will the teachers have time for my kids if Jason comes?" Jeanne had a meeting and had everyone come and talk about how it would be a wonderful learning experience for their children and at Playhouse we accept people where they are. I remember sitting, standing, or doing whatever I was doing as a co-op parent, listening to Jeanne talk to the children before Jason came. And she was telling them that Jason is different than they are, he can't see and so someone will have to take his hand and bring him over to the block area to play. And Jason doesn't talk and so when he wants more juice at snack or more cookies, he may bang his cup on the table and that's how we'll know that Jason wants more. It was such a beautiful way of describing it. Then Jason came and he was very impaired – it wasn't that he was just blind. And the parents were saying that he doesn't belong here and all of that. This is where Jeanne helped educate parents. Who was feeling they were neglected? Was it the parents or was it their children? You can kind of look at the other children and see what they are getting out of it. And Jason stayed.

Jason's inclusion in the classroom benefited all involved, including the other children and their families.

Although these ideals and practices seem obvious, they are actually quite challenging to employ. Through my thirty plus years as a teacher committed to social justice and later as a teacher educator, I have worked with schools and organizations who strive for diversity in terms of their student and teacher populations and who attempt to teach about acceptance. Unfortunately, too often these communities cannot walk their talk. They have strong values, but they have trouble putting them into practice. Constructing an integrated school involves risk, persistence, and creativity. Differences can lead to disagreement and unpredictable discussions, which often make people uncomfortable. I know this is true because my conversations about race, class, gender, sexual orientation, ability, and religion with our friends can even make Mark feel anxious. But in order to prepare our children to be advocates for others and not just bystanders who watch their friends be teased, made fun of, or even bullied, we have to have those challenging conversations with them. None of us are naturally equipped with the narratives to be inclusive. We have to practice them and sometimes we will make mistakes. Edie told the following narrative about a discussion that she observed in Ronnie Stern's class, which demonstrates the ways that teachers can model this thought process:

> There were three kids at a table having snack and a child said to another child, "I don't want to play with you. She's my friend and you're not." Ronnie Stern stopped and said, "You know. I know a child whose heart was so big that that child could have one friend, two friends, three friends …" I thought she wasn't telling them that they had to play together. She was just giving them another way to see the world that was a more inclusive way. That happened over

and over again – those types of things at Playhouse.

Being accepting of others is something that you work at continually. Playhouse has been doing it for fifty-six years.

Finding Your Own Playhouse

What sorts of characteristics should you look for to find a preschool that is committed to diversity? Here are some easy identifiers:

1. Visit the school and take a look at the makeup of the classes, in terms of both the children and the teachers. At Playhouse, at least one-third of the children in each class were children of color and about one-third of the teachers in the entire school were teachers of color. If diversity is an important principle, you should be able to see it.

2. Examine the images of children and families that decorate the walls. Are these images diverse? What about the toys, dolls, puzzles, games, music, videos, and other instructional materials? Do they represent different cultures, religions, languages, and families?

3. Peruse the libraries in the classrooms or school. Does the literature represent a variety of cultures and traditions?

4. Ask the school if you can attend parent/board meetings. You will get a good sense of the parent community by seeing who is involved in the running of the school. Look for a parent board that represents many different perspectives.

5. Inquire about policies such as recruitment, admissions, and sliding scale tuition. These administrative mechanisms will

give you insights into the commitment of the school.

6. Be careful not to mistake token celebrations for an authentic exploration of cultures. For example, simply sharing different foods can be superficial unless there is also discussion about their significance. It is fun to make latkes for Hanukkah, but more importantly I would want to talk about why they are traditional food for Jewish families in December.

7. Simply talking about African-Americans during Black History Month is not a multicultural curriculum. The school should infuse all discussions with examples of people from many different races and ethnicities in whatever open-ended topic the teachers are examining. Some topics that lend themselves to these conversations include community, family, traditions, peace, inventions, and story.

8. Another big red flag for me is when teachers and/or schools preach that they approach all children in the same way and that they don't see color. Claiming to be color blind or blind about any difference negates the existence of racism or any other ism. I want children to be accepting of others who are different and be aware that any discrimination is unacceptable. I agree with Vivian Paley when she writes "You Can't Say, You Can't Play."

9. I value schools that are willing to raise difficult issues with children, because these types of critical conversations raise awareness. Too often teachers shy away from ethical topics that do not have easy answers, fearing that they will get into uncharted territory. But kids are natural philosophers. They like to think about big abstract ideas like fairness or compassion, and they are still young enough to share

what they really think and feel rather than censoring their responses to conform to society. Modeling how to debate or disagree is essential.

10. Remember that schools committed to diversity have to continually work on it. No school is perfect, and tensions and conflicts do occur, especially in communities that represent many – even at Playhouse. The key is the willingness of the staff to engage in those difficult discussions.

CHAPTER FOUR

THE DEAD LADYBUG, THE WHITE LEOPARD, AND THE ARCHEOLOGIST: AUTHENTIC CHILD-CENTERED LEARNING AND PROBLEM POSING

But the child, unhampered, does not waste time. Not a minute of it. He is driven constantly by that little fire burning inside him, to do, to see, to learn. You will not find a child anywhere who will sit still and idle unless he is sick – or in a traditional classroom … Childhood's work is learning, and it is in his play … that the child work at his job. (Pratt, 1948, p. 7)

In many preschool contexts, children are expected to learn within a curriculum that is either driven by the teachers, predetermined, or even purchased. They are required to adopt pre-defined student behaviors rather than act as individuals. Teachers set the learning objectives for the day and the children follow the rigid plan, regardless of how they are feeling, where their interests lie, or whether they encounter a problem. Playhouse provides a much different type of environment, one where the individual interests and questions of children drive the curriculum, learning, and play. The curriculum evolves based on the individual interests and needs of the students and the staff. The teachers develop units that build on the questions and curiosity of the children. They understand that the children are "little scientists" who are able to construct their own knowledge with the support and scaffolding of teachers, parents, and classmates. The curriculum is not one size fits all but rather it is tailored to meet the needs and interests of the children. At Playhouse children are seen as individuals with unique learning styles and intelligences. Children are invited to explore, experiment, and inquire about problems that have emerged in their lives. They are encouraged to do so in their authentic play as well as through the use of art, music, science, mathematics, literature, and movement. The *process* of learning is the focus rather than the end product.

The teachers at Playhouse teach from a humanistic approach, drawing from their own lived experiences and instincts when they interact and respond to the children. They are unique because they possess dispositions of openness, caring, and reflectiveness. They prioritize listening to the children rather than talking at them. They understand that learning is not the transmission of knowledge from an all knowing adult to an unknowing child. They are flexible and understand that there is no right way of approaching an idea. They value and promote various questions and perspectives from children. This means that teachers may have to learn about new things in order to support the learning of their students. Moving into uncharted waters is sparked by the authentic need of students. As Jeanne Ginsberg explains, "We understand that spontaneous learning is authentic and experience based, and therefore we at

Playhouse are flexible in our teaching practices and look for and draw upon teachable moments."

My children, Michael and Griffin, are very different in the ways that they approach the world. Michael is our thinker, the serious one who weighs the pros and cons of each move. He always seems to pause, assess the situation, and then take a step. Griffin is the polar opposite. He tends to jump into the world with passion and excitement. When he was born, he took such a large first breath it popped a hole in his lung. Trying to assure us that it was nothing to worry about, the Chinese pediatric pulmonologist at the hospital told us that it was a sign that he was going to be a person that embraced life with enthusiasm and energy. He is fearless and always up for an experience or activity. He is definitely our risk taker. With two such different kids, one would think that Playhouse might only work for one but not the other. But, on the contrary, Playhouse was the perfect school for each of them because of its focus on building and developing curriculum that emerges from the questions and problems of individual children.

The Dead Ladybug

Playhouse teachers notice what is on the minds of the kids. They are "kidwatchers" (Goodman, 1996) by watching how they learn and actively listening to children and the many stories that they share from home. This occurs informally as the children are playing in the classroom or in more formal settings like circle time, which is a sort of class meeting time. The key is that Playhouse teachers invite stories, sending a message to the children that their experiences are valued and important.

Griffin tended to share many more stories from home than

Michael. Griffin, as an extremely verbal and social child, enjoyed circle time and always had something to contribute to the discussion. He still is very much the same today. Just a few weeks ago, his new Language Arts teacher remarked that she appreciated that he is always willing to participate. When he was three years old, two significant incidents occurred. First, during the summer before school started, he caught a ladybug and played with it, allowing it climb up and down his arm, before accidentally killing it. This incident, though it might seem minor to most adults, had a great impact on him. He became fascinated with death, and repeated his story over and over again, trying to make sense of it through the retelling.

Later that fall, Papa, his great-grandfather, passed away. Griffin spent months processing this death. He talked about who dies, how people die, and when people die. He tried to understand why his great-grandfather had died and not his great-grandmother. He asked if I was going to die soon. He said, "Old men die, but not old women. You know, my Papa died, but my Grandma Shirley is still alive."

Maria, his teacher, listened to both of these stories intently and she tried to find ways to explore death with the whole class. She did not shy away from the death discussion as many adults do, because they perceive death as too serious to discuss with kids. She understood that Griffin needed time to process these significant occurrences in his life. She found books to share about death, she talked about the cycle of life using the example of animals as well as people, and she used the seasonal changes as a metaphor for life and death. She asked other children to share their own sadness about loss. She invited his concerns and grief to become part of the classroom curriculum. By paying attention to Griffin, she was better able to connect with him, ask questions to help him process, and identify with him. "You know, Griffin, I know how you feel. I was really sad when my grandma died, too." Maria found a way to extract learning from a painful experience, and the curriculum became grounded in Griffin's needs and interests. In another school, the teacher might have been afraid to talk about death with young children – for many people, death is considered a taboo topic.

And believe it or not, after interviewing lots of Playhouse parents, I discovered that the topic of death was often part of the curriculum, because this concept frequently emerges for young children. Edie saved this list of definitions from her 1988 kinder-garten class:

Dead is …

Adam: You're up in the sky and you'll never come alive again.

Alex: Your body's no good anymore, but your spirit is still good.

Jordan: Only your bones are left.

Marshall: Your body is dead but things are still good.

Raj: Your life is good again.

Bruce: Your bones are still good.

Tyler: You don't come back alive.

Robyn: You're buried in the ground.

Garrett: Your skin is dried out, you can't come back alive if you don't believe in reincarnation.

Ilana: Someone's underground. Your heart stop beating, you could die.

Jarret: You couldn't live longer if you didn't get sick.

Alex: Dead is dead.

Playhouse: A Child-Centered Curriculum

At Playhouse, as Carolyn Rothschild described, "The child is the curriculum … The materials are so selected and the structure of the rooms are so set up to serve the child instead of the child serving the room or material." This involves allowing the questions and concerns of children to drive classroom inquiry (Dewey, 1943). Dewey believed that classrooms should be laboratories that contained "the materials, the tools with which the child may construct, create, and actively inquire" (p. 32).

For Griffin, his questions about death moved from his individual concern to the source of an authentic learning experience for the entire class. The flexibility of the teachers and the curriculum at Playhouse allowed my son's question to become the focus of the group. Too often teachers are so tied to the sequence of their lesson plans that they are fearful of divergence. In a child-centered curriculum where the child takes center stage, their interests and experiences become the catalyst for the teaching. Concepts and objectives emerge from interactions with the child. Edie Weiner describes the Playhouse concept of child centered curriculum. She reflects:

I think it was really just tuning into children … I think that Jeanne's focus was the child and it was always the child. What is it that makes this child this way and how can we help him? What is he needing? What's going on with him? It wasn't about product. It was always about process … Clean-up is still part of the program. Clean up isn't just to get the toys away. It is one more period in the day … for teachers it's putting the toys away to move on to the next activity as opposed to that in itself being valuable, being a teachable moment. So I think that was her focus always. It was not the program and it was not the materials. It was the child.

Not only are their concerns and questions validated, but at Playhouse, children are listened to. As Jeanne reflected:

They need to try things out themselves so there is a lot of movement in the school. Children need physical move-ment. There has to be a lot of language, talking to each other, talking to themselves, thinking out loud. There is a constant hum which is important … Learning is active. It's not inactive because learning is two way all the time. Children don't sit down and just … you're not filling up something. We feel the best teaching is done when you extract something from the child what he has and helping him to understand his perceptions and coping with it, not only perceptions but feelings first.

Children need to be given the chance to explore their hypoth-eses instead of being told that their thinking is incorrect. They need to be invited to make meaning for themselves rather than instructed on how to make sense of things. Ronnie Stern, a former parent and teacher at Playhouse from 1969 to 1979, illustrates this practice with great detail through the following story:

We would be digging for rocks. The big shovels, the real tools, the real work, not plastic. This is how it is set up, so it will work this way. So dig up the rocks, now we're going to weigh them, we're going to load them in wagons, we're going to drag them around, we're going to feel how heavy they are, we're going to paint them, we're gonna glue them, and so on. So I said, "Where did these rocks come from?" A child said, "The squirrels brought them," and I said, "Good thinking, because squirrels really bring a lot of stuff in here." Another child said, "No. The rocks fell down from the trees." A third thought, "A dump truck came in and dumped them." I summarized, "All good, good, good. From the information you have, you are making a very good connection and a very good educated guess."

Ronnie continues, explaining why allowing children to interpret the world is important:

In another school, someone would tell them, no, back hundreds of years ago, the glacier came across the earth and the rocks and the blah blah blah. Not necessary. Because it's about thinking and retrieving and making that web of facts and feeling good about risking an answer. That's the whole thing. Well, when people come in sometimes and ask, "Is this a school for my child?" someone has to explain to them that you don't have to give the correct answer. This is a laboratory for thinking. And that's all. Every idea is worthy.

In a thinking lab, you have the children observe things and make their own conclusions. Fran Miller shared another example of this: "You tell the kids to watch the wheels of a car and let us know what you see rather than telling the kids an explanation of the wheels."

The White Leopard and the Archaeologist: Exploration and Problem Posing Pedagogy

> As adults we often step in too quickly and try to "fix" problems or disputes. Step back and wait. Often children will find their own solutions to the problem if we just give them the chance. In the process we give them an opportunity to learn problem solving and a sense of autonomy. (Jeanne Ginsburg)

Michael did not always want to do the activities that the teachers proposed at Playhouse, but when he was able to create an activity on his own, it usually kept his interest for hours. (Funnily, he is still very much that way!) One day when he was four, he brought a small plastic white leopard to school. I always remembered it as a white tiger, but when I read this story aloud to Michael the other day, he corrected me: "I remember that day, Mom. It was a white leopard." Children at Playhouse are discouraged from bringing toys from home to avoid competition and commercial materials, but Maria, Michael's teacher, tended to be on the more relaxed side about these rules and the leopard seemed to have slipped by her purview.

During outdoor time, in the playground behind the school where the children usually go at least twice a day no matter the weather, Michael decided to dig in the sandbox. In true Playhouse style, the playground equipment is simple and accessible to the children, and invites the use of their imagination. The medium-sized rectangular sandbox offers the children the opportunity to engage with kitchen utensils, trucks, buckets, and shovels. The sandbox was definitely one of Michael's favorite spots. He enjoyed digging, burying things, and moving his fingers through the cool sand. On that particular spring day, Michael decided to bury the leopard and then find it and dig it up. He did this over and over again, enjoying that tedious repetitive hide-and-seek activity of which adults often tire but four-year-olds never seem to grow weary.

On his third round of "bury and excavate," the leopard seemed to disappear. Michael grew more and more frustrated, especially when Maria and Amy announced that it was time to go back into the classroom. He could not bear the idea of having to leave his beloved leopard buried deep in the sand. He was determined to stay on the playground until he found it. The pressure grew again when my friend Laura showed up midway through the day to take Michael to his gymnastics class. Although he has grown up with her and she is practically his aunt, her presence did not comfort him. Michael became more and more upset. There was no way he was going to abandon his beloved leopard. Rather than dismiss his concern and frustration, Maria, Anat, and Jessica – his teacher and the two school administrators – sat down with Michael and tried to understand his frustration, sadness, and resistance. If he had been at another school, I do not know whether this would have happened. Once he began to trust them and he felt like they were really listening to his concerns, he calmed down.

Rather than insisting that he follow the rest of the class, the Playhouse faculty asked him to think with them about possible solutions to the problem. Instead of digging around randomly in the sandbox, which had begun to feel as large as the beach at the Jersey Shore, they asked him to think about what an archaeologist might do in this case. They shared that archaeologists often excavate to find things and that perhaps they could use a grid method to make the process easier. They turned a very difficult situation into a teachable moment and they helped Michael to redirect his focus away from being frustrated to concentrating on making a grid out of the sandbox. Maria returned to her classroom and Anat and Jessica spent a good part of the afternoon with Michael as archaeologists. Together, they made a grid of the area where he thought the leopard was buried and began to look for it in small squares. The process was tedious, but the reward was enormous. It seemed that Michael appreciated that his concerns were taken seriously and that he was being listened to. It didn't hurt that he found the leopard, too!

At Playhouse learning looks different than it does at most traditional schools. The teachers understand that problem posing learning and exploration necessitates an atmosphere of respect and purpose. To do this, adults and children need to know one another well and develop trust. It also requires real time to allow for students to own their learning, acknowledge their progress, and solve problems for themselves. As Sizer (2004) writes, "Learning is not efficient" (p. 5). Exploring new ideas and solving real problems cannot be neatly placed into a lesson plan during a 45 minute block. Authentic learning is messy and it may involve expanded time for play, investigation, and reflection. What does this look and sound like? At her interview, Carolyn Rothschild, one of the founding parents, described this teaching paradigm in the following way:

> Children need to try things out for themselves so there is a lot of movement in the school. There has to be a lot of language, talking to each other, talking to themselves, thinking out loud. There is a constant hum. I think I need to say that because, for some people quiet is such a virtue.

And since no two children are alike, how they approach a problem will differ. When students' curiosity becomes the driving force of the curriculum, then the role of the teacher becomes one of coach – who provides materials, asks provocative questions, and encourages children to make decisions about their own learning.

In a child centered classroom, anything and everything has the potential to be explored. Ronnie Stern remembered that when her children attended Playhouse in 1969, there was endless play, a lot of messiness, and some smelliness too. She recalls:

> The kids I remember, I remember them doing cute things, and I remember them playing endlessly. And I remember the animals, and the dirt, and nobody sprayed any disinfectant. Oh my god, it was smelly. We used to talk about the smells, children should smell smells. We don't need deodorant or cleaning products. So that was very formative.

Although it is a funny memory of Playhouse, it speaks to the notion that at Playhouse there are very few boundaries about what can and cannot be discussed, explored, and investigated. Dirt and smells are all a part of the real world exploration. This is true in terms of all of the materials that the children explored including the playground equipment. Edie Weiner recalled Jeanne's guidelines for the playground:

> Jeanne was very adamant about not wanting stationary things in playground. She wanted things that children could move and create, use their imagination so they had these large boards and oil barrels that parents had donated and were cleaned and painted and everything. The kids would make pirate ships. They would make houses – they would make whatever they were thinking about at the time. There were forts … it was just so beautiful. You would come in and it would be a different thing because they would just move things around and create them.

Learning is an active embodied process where children need to move their bodies. It does not occur when children are sitting quietly in their seats. Teachers are not filling them with information – children make meaning for themselves when they are actively engaged in learning.

Sadly, in most schools, a more traditional model of schooling prevails and is in stark contrast to the Playhouse experience. Teachers generally have very rigid objectives and goals with standardized tests for which to prepare, and there are expectations of conformity and uniformity. In fact, that same spring, when Michael attended the kindergarten orientation at our local elementary school in Verona, he had an experience that signaled to us that regular school might be pretty different from Playhouse.

As part of a well-intentioned practice, all incoming kindergarteners are invited to a short orientation at the school. The children meet the kindergarten teachers, do an activity, and then sit on the rug, sing songs, and listen to a story. Although I did not witness this incident, Michael adamantly shared it with me on our walk home. Each child was asked to wear a nametag to facilitate the discussion with the teachers. This sounded like an excellent practice – I always encourage my students to get to know their students' names as quickly as possible as a way to build community. But in this case, the children were asked to wear their nametags on their chests. Michael (always the nonconformist) insisted instead on wearing his nametag on his back. He thought it was cooler and not as distracting. The teacher neither found this amusing nor tolerated the behavior. She immediately asked him to move his nametag to the front of his shirt, which caused Michael to become agitated. He did move the nametag to satisfy the teacher, but in order to preserve his individuality he refused to sing the song. He silently protested the call to conform and felt pleased and proud that he was able to do his own thing in true Playhouse spirit, even if the teacher had no idea!

I am not advocating anarchy in the classroom, but we know that children are more likely to learn when they are engaged in authentic experiences. This type of child-centered teaching is challenging for teachers. It is a lot easier for them to develop a curriculum in isolation from the children in their class. It is also easier to expect students to behave uniformly rather than to appreciate their individuality, but what are the effects of these decisions? Do we want to nurture children into adults who are thinkers, initiators, risk-takers, and leaders? Who are able to use strategies to cope with difficult situations? Or would we prefer to create adults who are rule-bound, dependent followers? In order to create a child-centered curriculum which fosters authentic learning, teachers have to approach children as individuals.

Finding Your Own Playhouse

What does a preschool look like that allows curriculum to emerge from the children? Here are some practices to look for:

1. Look for a school where in the morning, the teachers greet each child by name and welcome him/her into the classroom. Griffin loved arriving at Playhouse, partly because he so looked forward to being greeted by Maria and her warm hugs!

2. The school should feel inviting to children. The classrooms should have a lot of light, be decorated in bright colors, and be roomy. At Playhouse, Griffin would eagerly run into school and remark, "Mom, it smells like Playhouse!" when we entered, as if the scent of school was like that of

Grandma's house – warm, familiar, and inviting.

3. The classroom should be organized at a child's level. The cubbies, shelves, tables, chairs, toilets, and even posters should be accessible to kids. I learned so much from Playhouse about organizing spaces for kids. To this day, Michael and Griffin have their own basket cubbies at home where they keep hats, gloves, fleeces, shin guards, and baseball gloves.

4. Look for a child-centered classroom with a variety of learning centers that contain materials encouraging open exploration. Some possible learning centers could include building with blocks, dramatic play, art, science, library, math/logic, music, movement, and listening.

5. When you visit a preschool, ask what a typical day might entail. Make sure that there are unstructured times during the day when the children can choose their activities at different learning centers. Also, look for preschools that have outdoor time no matter the weather.

6. Look for preschools that use non-commercial books, materials, and toys. Ideally these materials and toys should also be made from natural sources.

7. There is so much to learn from nature. A child-centered preschool uses class pets, plants, sand, water, and the great outdoors to encourage questioning and curiosity.

8. You want to find classrooms where kids are invited to explore open-ended art materials. Their art experiences should not feel like cookie-cutter crafts where they have to follow specific directions to create a generic final product.

You want them to have a chance to experiment with different textures, colors, materials, etc. and invent! Griffin and Michael are so inventive that I sometimes wish I had a room just to store all of their many creations and masterpieces.

9. Ask the school staff how they develop curriculum for the classes. You want to hear that they pay close attention to the children's interests, needs, and strengths. Some popular themes explored at this age are dinosaurs, the fire station, seeds and plants, insects, robots, and space. Ideally the school will ask you about your child's interests before the school year even begins.

10. You will be looking for teachers who develop positive relationships with children. This could involve playing, eating, sharing stories, and cleaning up with them, or reading, talking, and listening to them. This is easy to look for, especially during snack or lunch times.

11. Child-centered teachers invite children to call them by their first names and physically get down on their level. They engage with the kids in peaceful and non-confrontational ways. This sends the message to the children that there is mutual respect. It may sound ridiculous, but I am always a bit put off when I enter a preschool where the teachers insist on being called by their last names.

12. You will know that teachers are spending a lot of time kidwatching if you see them sitting on the floor with the children and engaging in play. At Playhouse, Maria would often sit alongside Michael and help him to build a train track or partake in Griffin's dinosaur family road trip.

13. Child-centered teachers invite children to ask questions and share different perspectives and opinions rather than expecting them to give the one "right" answer. They will ask such questions as "Does anyone else want to add what they see?" or "What do you think is going to happen next?"

14. They offer options to students so that they can make choices for themselves and feel empowered.

15. Playhouse teachers form connections with children by sharing personal experiences with them – this humanizes the adults. This was especially evident in Griffin's classroom experience after his great-grandfather had passed away, when Maria expressed sadness about her own loss. They make comments that indicate a shared feeling, such as "I love that story, too."

16. Finally, children need to have opportunities to struggle. Open-ended activities that invite kids to encounter problems and devise solutions allow for struggle. Too often we parents want to solve the problems for our children.

CHAPTER 5

LISTENING, SEEING, AND UNDERSTANDING CHILDREN: DEVELOPING A POSITIVE SELF-CONCEPT WITHIN A CLASSROOM COMMUNITY

The central philosophy is one of enhancing, nurturing, and developing what the child brings to the school. It's helping the child understand himself and starting there. For each child, helping him identify with his needs, wants, his pleasures, and his skills and making him feel worthwhile … Everything else feeds into that … helping a child develop a good self-image, feeling like a worthwhile person, developing self confidence in a setting which allows for things to happen so that he can understand his motives, himself. The program is adjustable, flexible so that the teachers can use the program to feed that central aim so that it will be very flexible because each child is different. (Carolyn Rothschild, founding parent)

At Playhouse there is an intentional emphasis on helping children to develop self-knowledge and a positive self-concept in an environment that promotes the awareness of the needs of others and the larger community. Children are valued as individuals and are seen, heard, and understood, rather than seen and not heard. They are invited to be self-reflective, to develop self-confidence, and to appreciate their own uniqueness. They are encouraged to understand and accept themselves, and to be able to articulate any and all feelings. They are guided by teachers to discover personal strategies to comfort themselves and recognize and cope with all sorts of feelings like anger, frustration, and disappointment, so that they can successfully self-regulate their emotions and behaviors.

Through play and discussion with teachers, other students, and parents, children are encouraged to express their needs and actively develop the language and tools to negotiate, compromise, and share as democratic citizens of a learning community. Teachers model feeling language and ask open ended questions to provide scaffolding for these types of conversations. Also children are allowed to have second choices so that they never feel stuck or forced to do something with which they are not comfortable. This happens naturally and organically in Playhouse classrooms because they are constructed as safe spaces where everyone can talk about difficult issues, think critically, take a stand, and take risks while learning. Children examine problems, questions, and challenges from multiple perspectives, and there is never an emphasis on just one way of thinking about an issue, or on just one "truth" for that matter.

Unlike many preschools and schools, the curriculum and structures at Playhouse are malleable, and are organized in ways that adapt to the students' needs rather than forcing children to conform to a set program. The school is designed to meet a variety of needs for a variety of different children. As Carolyn Rothschild reflects:

> I think most schools have a program and children come into it and they have to fit into it. We have children coming in to bend the school, stretch the school to meet the needs of that child. I think that is the difference. It's just a matter of making the shoe fit the foot rather than the foot fit the shoe.

In order to do this well, teachers have to pay particularly close attention to children. They have to listen to their narratives and conversations, they have to "kidwatch" and observe their behaviors, and they have to be open to allowing the curriculum, questions, and even materials to emerge from the needs and interests of the children.

This is complex and challenging work for the teacher – and is also a much more demanding type of teaching than preparing a pre-set curriculum and materials. Rothschild reminds us that "the best teaching is done when you extract something from the child" and help her to articulate, acknowledge, and understand her feelings and perceptions about it. This requires creating a platform or a stage where children can express their feelings safely, whether positive or negative, without fear of judgment or consequence. Inviting children to know themselves and express how they are feeling leads to understanding how to self-control and make productive decisions about how to live socially, in a community where there are needs of others to be considered. Recognizing one's feelings and determining if they will get in the way of social interactions with peers or adults or learning is essential, and that process takes much practice. I know plenty of adults who still have not mastered this kind of self-knowledge, and as a result they walk around feeling angry, sad, or disappointed.

Mirroring the Feelings of Children

What does this look like in practice? Jeanne continually reminds me of the influence that Dorothy Baruch (1939) had on her approach to teaching children. She recalled that Baruch recommended that teachers and parents "mirror the feelings of the child." To Jeanne, that means that "if a child was feeling something, the teacher should say it, repeat it, and mirror their feelings so they understand that you know what they're saying." By acknowledging their feelings, and mirroring them, the children begin to see that these feelings are real and that they are okay to have. Edie Weiner illustrates this stance with the following example:

> When a kid was angry, there was no yelling. You could talk to them about their angry feelings. Maybe you'd sit down and make a book with them about the things that make them angry and they could add to it. It's not denying children their emotions, what they feel. There were all of those special ways of treating a child without getting angry. If a teacher felt, "Oh my God. I've had it," Jeanne would put the focus on the child. What does the child need? How can we help? She got you to start thinking about that child in different ways than the traditional way, the management way. It compelled you as a teacher because it felt like you were doing more than just teaching. You were really making a difference.

Edie contrasts this stance with others that she has seen as a social worker, where professionals deny the emotions of children. She recalls:

> I remember being at the therapeutic nursery that I'm affiliated with and actually listening to one of the teachers who's

now a psychologist. She was up on the roof because in New York City, playgrounds are on the roof. These are children who have deficits and this little girl was going, "I don't like the wind! I don't like the wind!" This teacher is looking over at her and saying, "Yes you do. You like the wind." And I'm thinking, "No she doesn't. Why are you denying her her reality?" Rather than saying to her, "Yes. It's windy and you're not liking it. Is there a place you could be where it would be less windy?"

Mirroring feelings involves recognizing and articulating the feelings that children are experiencing – of giving a voice to those feelings and giving the children some ownership over those feelings. Parent Helen Strauss shared this anecdote about coming upon a little girl at Playhouse who was painting out her anger:

I was dropping my kids off at Playhouse and I could see inside that there was one child with a big paint brush in her hand and there was an easel with white newsprint, nothing on it. This kid was obviously very angry and she dipped the brush in black paint and went "grrrrrrrr." The paint just sort of drizzled down, slowly, peacefully and when it did that, she sort of became peaceful too. She was identifying with what the paint was doing and it took the anger out of her. I said to myself, "This is one for the books – how impressionable and accepting a child can be in an environment she doesn't understand, doesn't need to understand. It's just there and she's part of it."

Finding ways to invite children to express their emotions also allows them to think of how to take action to make things better for themselves or to problem solve. This opposes how too often in society we are quick to deny children and adults their feelings. We insist that people are not sad or not angry or not frustrated and we let these emotions fester.

Developing a Positive Self-Concept

Both Michael and Griffin greatly benefitted from the focus on developing a positive self-concept, and having opportunities to tune in to their emotions and really know themselves. I can recall multiple incidents not only when they were at Playhouse, but also several years later where this self-knowledge helped them to navigate difficult situations or make decisions about their own well-being. For example, when Griffin was five and in Maria's class, he came home one day and announced that he didn't go into circle time. He said he had been feeling angry and upset and he had needed some time on his own. He recognized his emotions, realized that they would get in the way of his participation during circle time, and he self-regulated. It was not a time out. Maria was not making the decision for him. He was not being punished. He was simply choosing what was best for him in that moment.

This was often the case for Michael too. One summer when he was 5, he attended a sports summer camp instead of completing another summer at Playhouse. I thought that it would be good for him to be in a more "typical" setting, especially as we were gearing him up for kindergarten in our local neighborhood public school. He seemed relatively content there which was partially why I was surprised to receive a phone call from the counselor. What could have happened? Was everything okay? She called to tell me that she was concerned because Michael was refusing to play softball and she interpreted his behavior as defiant. I was so surprised, in part because he loved physically playing with other children and he never shied away from sports. When I picked him up later that afternoon, I got the whole story. He wasn't being defiant – he simply did not want to play a game where there were winners and losers. He had always been highly competitive and he truly hated losing – who doesn't? He knew that at the end of the game there would be winners and losers, and that the winners would be rewarded with candy. He said, "Mom. I didn't want to get upset if I lost so I didn't want to play the game." Rather than being defiant, he was self-regulating. He knew himself well enough to know how he might react to losing and he made a decision. When I tried to explain this to the counselor the next day, she just did not get it. It was then I realized that Playhouse has done wonders for Michael. He had the tools to know himself well, express how he felt, and make the right choices. And of course that was the last summer he went to that camp.

In truth both Michael and Griffin are still very much this way. Last year, as a sophomore in high school, Michael and I met with the guidance counselor in preparation for the college application process. We had had one of those stressful mornings where we were running late, Michael couldn't find a textbook he needed, and we were bickering. I was anxious about how the meeting would go and then, as so often is the case, there was a completely different Michael in the meeting. He was still somewhat shy but he had something to say. The guidance counselor asked questions to try to get to know him and he very clearly stated what he hoped to study and be. He said something like: "I want to design things, preferably video games. I want to think in three dimensions and I want to use a mixture of computer programming and art." The guidance counselor seemed impressed. She couldn't believe how clear and focused he was, and she remarked as such. She said, "You really know yourself Michael. That is really going to help you in the long run."

Griffin is the exact same way. About a year ago, he was begging me to get him a piccolo for Christmas. I was sort of hedging: "Griffin you already have lessons in percussion and bassoon. You have a vocal coach and you are in several productions. You have a basement filled with instruments – keyboard, drum set, various percussion instruments. How can you take on something else? What is the point?

He very seriously replied: "Mom, I think it's time you face the fact that this – performing arts – is what I want to do with my life. I want to be a performer whether it is an actor, singer, or musician. I will be working in a theater. You just have to get used to it."

Now what was I to say? He was right. Would we really deny him a piccolo if he showed interest? And for about nine months he took piccolo lessons. Those are my boys. They are Playhouse kids. They have good self-images and they know themselves. It doesn't make their lives easier, but it allows them to live their own truths.

My children's stories of the impact of a positive self-concept echo many of the stories that the founding parents have shared about their own children and their children's peers. For example, I remember one parent Carol Lewis talking about her son who liked to listen to music. He used to sit by the record player all day and listen to music. Carol grew concerned about it – worrying that he needed to do a variety of activities – and approached Jeanne about it. But Jeanne's response was "That's what he needs to do now." Many years later this same young man wrote a musical score for a Broadway play. Edie reflects:

So, how do you know what it is that a child needs or doesn't need? I think a belief in letting children kind of direct themselves is an important part of that, but not always. I think there are times when children get stuck and you need to help them along the way.

Edie also recalls the following scenario about her own son:

I remember when my son was here, there was a child who was difficult and I remember my little son coming home and saying, "Dougie had to sit by himself today." I said, "How come?" He said, "Because Dougie needs to learn how to like himself more."

Children at Playhouse not only develop their own self-concept but also learn to feel compassion for the others in the class. They begin to understand that self-regulating and figuring out our needs is part of becoming a member of a learning community. Similarly, Ronnie Stern recalls saying to her children, "You have your own brain. Someone else can say that's okay, but you know how you feel and that's fine." Much like my own apprehensions, she recognized that beating to your own drumbeat has some repercussions. She reflected:

It didn't make them as compliant as the school wanted them to be. They would love it at Playhouse, but nowhere else did a teacher love them because one of them could say I don't want to do that because it's boring. They would say it nicely but it was not well received.

Teachers who help their students to nurture positive self-concepts are consummate kidwatchers. They observe children and attempt to understand their strengths and needs. There is no judgment – this is a process of interpreting and understanding children. The following are poems that Jeanne wrote about a variety of different students. What is apparent is how she recognizes and values their individual personality traits and never positions these as deficient or negative. Here are a few of her poems:

You stood back a while
Standoffish was your immediate style
After much crying, then one day
Lo and Behold, you made it with clay
And paints and glue and instruments too
Then one day a voice heard
And without stopping, word after word
Till I had to say hold
You changed from shyness to bold.

A year of discovery without end
For self-help on mama you needn't depend
Buttons and zippers are a snap
Letters and numbers and colors too
Are a few of your favorite things to do
To get your feet on the ground and things off the shelf
You'll need to make decisions all by yourself.

Jill comes to school with a "Look I'm here."
Attitude of adventure, low in fear
Painting only exploring with shades
Vocabulary and phrases are on a par with the grades
Cast on leg her movements inspire
Here is a girl we all must admire.

Jon comes to school asking is it a cape day today?

You see superman is a big part of his play

His resistance is down

Smiles replace frown

Love of guinea pigs

Love of dancing

Jon makes music so entrancing!

Positive Discipline

Hand in hand with building a positive self-concept is using positive discipline. What does this involve? Discipline at Playhouse is based on four key tenets:

1. Teachers and children talk and listen to each other.

2. Teachers help children find their own solutions.

3. If children cannot find their own solutions, the teachers present options so that the child does not feel trapped. For example, teachers do not ask children why they acted inappropriately. Instead they use questions such as "Can you tell me *what* happened?" and "Can you tell me *how* it happened?"

4. Finally, if there are strong emotions, the teachers separate the child temporarily to give her a chance to cool down.

At Playhouse, the belief is that when children misbehave – as they do frequently – their behavior needs to be acknowledged, but not approved. Then rather than focusing on punishment, teachers need to help children understand the problem and not reprimand them. Often misbehavior means that the child is trying to tell us something. Playhouse teachers use a variety of strategies (including humor) to deflate the tension and emotion of a situation. More than anything else, at Playhouse adults do not solve conflicts for children. Rather they help them find their own solutions. This is especially important because the adult's behavioral expectations should correlate with the child's expectations of herself.

Carolyn Rothschild provides further explanation during her interview:

> This has to be self-discipline, meaning children learn how to set their own limits with help from the teacher. At Playhouse, the teacher really becomes a facilitator and helps the child first of all reflect, because she listens to the child, she reflects what she is saying so the child hears it again from the outside so she's able to confirm or deny. After this interaction, the teacher can show how a child can have other options for getting what he wants or what he needs when they're not acceptable so the child never feels trapped, stuck or dead-ended.

This can be a complex and messy process, because inviting three year olds to make decisions can feel risky. That is why the role of the teacher is so important. As Carolyn Rothschild continues:

> First of all, the teacher has to help the child see what is safe for her – safety for herself and others around her. That's one of the rules. Is that really safe? Children don't always know, can't make that determination.

Another scenario in a Playhouse classroom that would need teacher mediation might be when a child gains too much power and becomes bossy. Carolyn explains that:

Sometimes adults and other children will feed that power. And that's an area where a teacher would have to step in and be able to see that being too powerful in situations, bossing other people around is just not good for other people but not good for the child to carry that kind of power.

This is one of the challenges of being in a classroom environment where the children are free to express themselves. Sometimes the teachers have to help the children set or negotiate boundaries.

Conflicts are resolved differently at Playhouse. As I was researching for this book, I came across a Playhouse Handbook from 1967. There was a small section on positive discipline where there is a description of how if there is a problem between children, that besides comforting the child you feel has been attacked, you should also comfort and console the child who does the act. This approach was confirmed by multiple parents I interviewed. Charlie Rosen and Jeanne discussed some examples to illustrate this:

Charlie: When kids got very upset and would hit each other, Jeanne would be able to let both the hitter and the one who was getting hit know that she could understand what they were going through and that there are ways of managing it … It was the way to mediate. I'll give you another example. Two girls, sisters, wanted an orange. There was only one orange in the refrigerator, and they kind of fought over it. The mother says all right, pulls out a knife and cuts the orange in half, and gives one half to one of the kids and the other half to the other kid. That didn't satisfy either one of them. One of them wanted to have a whole orange to eat, and the other wanted the peel. She was using the peel for one thing or another, and she wanted the whole peel of the whole orange. Now if the mother had asked the kids what their interest was for the peel.

Jeanine: What the appeal was (laughs).

Charlie: Yeah, what they wanted out of this orange, it would have been solved much better, instead of cutting this orange and saying you have one part you have the other.

Edie Weiner gave this example of Jeanne's method of conflict resolution. She said in graduate school she met a professor who had sent his children to Playhouse. When he learned that Edie was the president there, he told this story:

> He told me a vignette about kids in the sandbox. He was a co-op parent at the time and another kid picked up a stone and hit a kid with it. Jeanne went and comforted the hitter who was so upset. That was the beauty of Playhouse. Somewhere else, the victim would have been the one. And the flipside of that is that rocks should never have been in the sandbox. And that was Playhouse too.

Finding Your Own Playhouse

What does a school look like where children are encouraged to develop self-confidence? Here are some practices for which you should look:

1. Look for a school where the children are welcomed and greeted in the morning. Both Michael and Griffin relished coming to Playhouse. They ran into school and immediately hugged Maria in the classroom.

2. Look for classrooms where the children are accepted for

who they are, where there are few rules, and where there is a sense that the school is interested in your child as an individual. Michael started Playhouse when he was only two and a half years old. At the time he loved drinking chocolate milk and although I knew it wasn't the healthiest drink, I was worried that taking it away as he transitioned to school would be difficult. Never once did the teachers or school administrators comment. They accepted the children with all their quirks and particularities and they loved them for those individual traits.

3. Find classrooms where children are invited to share their feelings, even when those feelings are negative or not conventional. Often this could be during circle time, but it also could take place during play time when teachers engage with children one on one.

4. Pay attention to the interactions between teachers and children. At Playhouse, teachers connect with children by sharing personal experiences to humanize adults, by making comments that indicate a shared feeling such as "I love that story too," and by praising students.

5. The children at Playhouse feel empowered and listened to because they have opportunities to make choices and share opinions. They are invited to construct their own worlds, and are acknowledged for the ways in which they think about those worlds.

6. To instill a sense of individual responsibility, children should have occasions to help themselves, such as through pouring juice, cleaning up, putting on coats and shoes, and washing hands. Michael and Griffin grew to be indepen-

dent at Playhouse. This independence transferred to their home lives, where they began to do such things as clean up after themselves, prepare their own snacks, and use the bathroom.

7. To develop a positive self-concept, children have to be praised in thoughtful ways. "Good job" can feel like an empty compliment that ends the interaction. It may feel good in the moment but it does not last. Asking a question like, "Well what do you think about it?" or making a comment like, "I really like how you used that bluish color to make the sky" can invite conversations and invite the child to judge for herself. This internal judgment is key.

8. Children also need to be allowed to struggle, even if it means becoming frustrated or angry. This is part of the process of getting to know themselves and what their emotional thresholds are.

CHAPTER 6

TOUCHED BY PLAYHOUSE WE ARE NEVER QUITE THE SAME: PARENTING THE PLAYHOUSE WAY

Playhouse children move with unknown grace, born of forgotten incidents … Mothers remember better. Then too, I remember a mother helped to find her children. I mean to look and really see them, and be glad. And anxieties turned to pleasure at the good things there in every child, and beginning that long slow road to motherhood, that vision of my child in every child. Touched by Playhouse we are never quite the same again. Teachers, mothers, fathers, children, small and grown. We never really leave this family, but where we go, we do things having these memories of a school and of a person who made possible that school. (Jessie Herdick, former Playhouse teacher)

These words illustrate beautifully the power of Playhouse. Unlike my own schooling experiences as well as those of Michael and Griffin's post preschool, "touched by Playhouse we," parents and children, "are never quite the same." The very purpose and organization of Playhouse is focused on nurturing a strong connection between the home and the school, which means that parents are also influenced by the schooling experience. I learned to really see and appreciate my children at Playhouse, and to parent in a thoughtful, accepting, and inquiry based way. This occurred through the many interactions I had at drop-off, in the classrooms, talking with the teachers, volunteering for field trips, attending Board meetings, organizing events, and generally being an active member in a cooperative school. Seeing my children for who they are was not a recipe with steps to follow – it was more of an approach, a stance, a way of looking at them. Rather than framing their quirky individual characteristics as negatives or as obstacles, Playhouse helped me to understand that these traits were a part of them and that I could differentiate my parenting to accommodate their individual and separate needs and build from their strengths. And since my time there I have used Playhouse as a touchstone whenever I am unsure of what to say or how to approach Michael and Griffin. It sounds magical but frankly Playhouse parenting is challenging because it requires intense kidwatching, great attention to detail, and emergent strategies. Rules are not set in stone, issues come up that need to be addressed, and there is no arsenal of tricks. These twists and turns of parenting are like any journey, with peaks and valleys, victories and losses, but in the end I always feel like I am at least striving to do the right thing by my children, and that is an enormous gift that I received from Playhouse – more than anyone else from Maria and Danielle (Playhouse teachers), Anat, and Jeanne.

As I described in Chapter Five, parenting that allows for the individuality of your child also necessitates the child having self-awareness and a positive self-concept. Again, I am quite certain that this is not always the agenda of most preschools, but at Playhouse it was one of the most important goals of their mission for children. As Alice Prager said:

> I really think that they just had a really good sense of themselves. I'm my own boss, remember that Jeanne? I'm my own boss, and how parents were misinterpreting that, what does that mean, aren't I his boss?

When your child is his or her own boss, then the role of the parent shifts more into being a facilitator. This requires listening, guiding, and supporting a child's decision making without of course letting them be in danger. This can be a difficult shift for parents as it is often not at all the way in which they were raised. It wasn't such a leap for me because this is exactly how my grandmother parented and it is very much how I strive to teach, but it is not what most people believe, including many teachers and administrators in public schools.,.

What has this looked like over the years? It was my observations of Michael at Playhouse as well as my discussions with his teacher Maria that helped me to understand that he was the type of child that had to make decisions for himself. As I have written in earlier chapters, we always considered Michael "the thinker" who would survey a situation, assess how he himself was feeling, and then carefully decide whether or not he wanted to participate in a group activity or join in with the whole class. For example, on a regular basis he would debate his participation in circle time. Michael was never 100% sure in the transitional moment if he wanted to join the larger group. So sometimes he would literally seat in his cubby and watch the class and then when he felt ready, in his body and mind, he would walk to the rug and join his friends. Watching

Maria allow him to take his time and make the decision for him-self was a significant parenting lesson for me. When I talked with her afterward, she would say "It's just circle time. We don't have to force him. It is more important that he has the chance to make the decision for himself. And if he doesn't join us, it doesn't really matter." But nine times out of ten he would enter the circle when he was ready.

Although not every parenting situation allows me to use this strategy, I think for Michael I have tried to invite him to make deci-sions for himself as much as possible. These are not easy conversa-tions to have, but I have always approached them with respect for his personhood. This has been especially true in high school when he is bombarded with homework all the time with a rigorous course schedule and band practice. My instinct has been to push him to get a little bit of homework done each day of the weekend so that on Sundays he is not overwhelmed with work, but he has decided on a different strategy. He relaxes and socializes with friends on Friday and Saturday evenings and then cranks work out on Sunday. Sometimes that means he stays up until 2:00 am, but his rationale is that he is completely exhausted from doing work all week and needs a substantial break to recharge. Again this is not how I would organize my own work and definitely not what I would choose for myself, but there is something incredibly empowering for him in making his own decisions and living with the consequences of those decisions. Michael knows himself well and is self-aware because of his years at Playhouse, an insight about him of which I am reminded time and time again by his high school counselor. He is comfort-able making decisions for himself and generally they work for him.

And Griffin? Well anyone who has ever met Griffin would tell you that he is confident and very comfortable marching to his own drum (and he's a drummer too!). I do not actually think it would be an exaggeration to say that he has exuded self-confidence since his Playhouse years. He has always had a particular clothing style and haircut that he picked for himself. He has been involved in acting since he was six years old and he has a particular affinity for animals – an interest that he shares with his dad who had an iguana living free range with him when we first met.

For years, he was obsessed with chickens and would beg to spend time at the Turtle Back Zoo visiting them. About 5 years ago, we were at a neighbor's barbecue and we started talking with a friend from Montclair who has chickens. I remember immediately introducing her to Mark and encouraging him to get us chickens. Next thing you know we had five chickens and a chicken coop in our backyard. This to me is a very good example of inquiry based parenting – I knew Griffin had an interest in chickens and I figured that it would be an excellent learning opportunity for Michael and him to have to care for them. They learned why and how chickens lay eggs, what their needs are in terms of food, water, and cleaning of the coop, and some more unexpected lessons like death when one of the chickens was eaten by a neighbor's cat, and disease when one of the baby chicks didn't make it. These are all important life lessons, and really paying attention to Griffin and Michael's interests have been our way of parenting.

This inquiry-based parenting has served our family well and the after-effects continue to appear as we are now preparing for the college process and Michael and Griffin's move from the high school. Our children know who they are and what they want from life. Although I realize that these goals and pathways may change, it is heartwarming and exciting to watch them have very specific interests and objectives and strive to achieve them. Michael is an interesting, creative, and innovative young man who has combined his interests in engineering and computer science with fantasy writing and art. He aspires to design video games, is an avid Dungeons and Dragons player, and plays the clarinet in the marching and concert bands. Griffin is a performer who juggles his time in plays and musicals, and plays percussion in the jazz band and bassoon in the concert band. Both of them know what their interests are, and they are not afraid to pursue them.

So much of the seeds of this foundation of a positive self-concept were planted at Playhouse, where they learned to trust their own voices and feel empowered. And this does not simply play out in terms of their own needs and desires. Having a positive self-concept also provides them with the confidence to take a stand and speak out when they feel others are being treated unfairly. This was the second valuable lesson that stayed with my children many years after their time at Playhouse.

Modeling A Commitment to Social Justice

Recently I had the opportunity to watch the movie *Loving* (2016) which is based on the true story about an interracial married couple, Richard and Mildred Loving, and their legal battle to be allowed to be married in the state of Virginia. Their marriage violated the state's anti-miscegenation statute, the Racial Integrity Act of 1924, which prohibited marriage between people classified as "white" and "colored." They were married in 1958 in Washington D.C. and were forbidden to live in Virginia as a married couple. In 1964, Mildred contacted Robert Kennedy who referred them to the American Civil Rights Union. In 1967, Loving v. Virginia was a landmark civil rights decision of the United States Supreme Court which invalidated state laws prohibiting interracial marriage.

As I watched the movie, I was struck by the fact that Playhouse was only in its 7th year when the Lovings were married. Granted the school was in New Jersey and not in Virginia, but it reminded me of how radical the founders of Playhouse really were. They had a serious commitment to making the school a place to nurture compassion and acceptance and they were unrelenting in making that commitment a reality. They recruited families of color from the moment they began, and although challenging they have carried on this tradition for the past 65 years. Walking their talk rather than simply have a philosophical stance, they established a sliding scale tuition knowing that this would allow a more diverse group of families to attend Playhouse. They understood that as the economy changed and the opportunities for women to work opened, they needed to change the design of the school and support families with two working parents. They created classroom options for children who needed all day school, like my own children, which they still have to this day. Once they were financially able to purchase a building for the school, they intentionally found a space in downtown West Orange because they felt it would locate them in a neighborhood of families from a variety of socioeconomic backgrounds. And finally their pillars and curriculum have always reflected their appreciation for all families. They were and continue to be devoted to what Mildred Loving's character insists when she says "We may lose the small battles, but win the big war" (*Loving*, 2016).

The Playhouse founders had "radical hope" a term that Junot Diaz (2016) borrows from Lear (2008). In the wake of a Trump presidency, Diaz wrote this in a piece in the *New Yorker*:

> But all the fighting in the world will not help us if we do not also hope. What I'm trying to cultivate is not blind optimism but what the philosopher Jonathan Lear calls radical hope.

"What makes this hope *radical*," Lear writes, "is that it is directed toward a future goodness that transcends the current ability to understand what it is." Radical hope is not so much something you have but something you practice, it demands flexibility, openness, and what Lear describes as "imaginative excellence." Radical hope is our best weapon against despair, even when despair seems justifiable, it makes the survival of the end of your world possible. Only radical hope could have imagined people like us into existence. And I believe that it will help us create a better, more loving future. (Diaz, 2016).

This article comforted me, as it did many others, but it also resonated deeply for me not only in terms of my own history of a grandmother deeply committed to the education of all children, but also with the radical Playhouse founders who in my eyes demonstrated their flexibility, openness, and Lear's "imaginative excellence". They understood that the only way to change the world was to actively construct a sustainable community that operationalized their core principles. Rather than spending their energy critiquing their options for their children, they took a large leap of faith and founded a school. They weren't sure what would happen and how it would all play out, but they had hope that they could make a mark on the world and do something different than what already existed. This is radical hope incarnate. It is what was needed in the 1950s and it is what is needed now. It is timeless.

The years spent at Playhouse for Michael and Griffin fueled their instincts about what was "normal" in their lives. They have a deep understanding that all people should be treated with respect, care, and compassion. Though so different, they engage in the world with a deep rooted acceptance of others. Michael does this more quietly, in his shy and introverted way. He was often the child in elementary school who would be asked to sit next to a child who had been teased or left out by others. He would smile and assure them with his patience and kindness. Whenever we visit friends with young children, even now with Michael towering over them, the littlest ones love to play with him. They find him comforting. My friend Laura's daughter, Annie, calls him "my prince." In 5th grade, which is in the middle school in Verona, he, like so many other tweens, was struggling to figure out who he was and why he was important. He felt upset that he wasn't the best athlete or the student with the best grades. My response to him is vivid in my memory. I said: "Your gift is that you are a very kind person. You don't judge other people and you try to accept everyone. You are diplomatic and you don't allow others to hurt people. This is a wonderful gift Michael and one that you should be very happy to have."

Griffin takes on his commitments to social justice quite differently. Since he was little, he has always felt for others. He has enormous amounts of empathy, a trait that we both recognize can be double-edged as sometimes he feels too much. In elementary school, he was concerned that the children who were taken out of class to receive speech therapy services were being discriminated against. He felt that it was unfair that they would be missing class time and that they would be singled out. When we were traveling in Jamaica about 5 years ago, he expressed concern about the children he saw on the side of the road who were walking barefoot. He asked why they didn't have shoes and if they were hungry. He has always accepted all people and has tried to be inclusive and open minded. More recently he traveled to New Orleans with his choir to perform *Joseph and the Technicolored Dream Coat* and do community service. He was completely comfortable both spending the night in the shelter, and preparing and serving meals to the homeless. He has used his outgoingness to speak and advocate for his peers and strangers alike. He has a sense of duty, of giving back to others, and I know these characteristics will serve him well in the coming years.

My children were not the only ones who were influenced by Playhouse. I too as a parent found my experiences there helped to strengthen my voice as an advocate for my children and others.

Parent Activism

Being an active parent at Playhouse, both in the classrooms and also on the Board and eventually as co-president, I too had opportunities to find my voice and advocate not only for my own children but also really for all children. The radical hope of the Playhouse founders has been contagious. Why simply complain about the policies that impact the lives of children in schools? Why not actively have a voice and speak out against the barrage of policies that are restricting their learning experiences? Playhouse gave Michael and Griffin a voice but I think to some degree it also helped me to strengthen my own voice.

This was the case for a variety of reasons. First, at Playhouse all parents are welcomed to participate in the school in whatever capacity they are able. Unlike most school settings, passive parenting is not encouraged. This invitation to be present in your child's school shifts the ways in which you think or your agency for your child. I knew that if Michael or Griffin had any issues or concerns that I should address them with their teachers. Playhouse has an open door policy. There are no secrets – parents just have a place in the school. I do not want to suggest that this made those sorts of conversations easy or that we all agreed all of the time, but I do think spaces were opened to have them unlike many of my experiences in public school. My voice was valued and heard. Additionally, the opportunities to contribute to the school community, whether through working in the library, attending the board meetings, or planning events made me feel like I had agency in the school. If there was something that parents felt needed to be changed or activities that needed to be added, we had a space to make those suggestions and actively work toward them. If we were concerned about the diversity of students for example, we actively strategized to attend town meetings where there were families of color. If we needed to raise funds for a slide for the playground, we thought through what we thought would be the best way to do that. Parents are an integral part of the school community and they are asked to partake in as many endeavors as they have time.

I also think that having the chance to raise my children in a community of like-minded people was an incredibly nurturing way to learn, through doing, how to parent. I felt like I was parenting in a larger collective, and if I made mistakes or stumbled, that there was a safety net of experts and peers to support me. Being part of this collective strengthened my voice as a parent activist because I never felt alone. I felt that I could take a stand and be vocal because others were behind me thinking and feeling the same thing.

So, just as the school's effects on the boys continue as they enter adolescence and adulthood, so too does the school's effects continue to influence me. This is where I found myself about two years ago when I noticed the increasingly heavy emphasis on test preparation and testing in my children's public schools. I had to do something – I could not just criticize it theoretically. I had to find a way to take a stand.

Because of my work in teacher education, I had spoken with several organizers like Michelle Fine and Stan Karp in Montclair who encouraged me to attend their *Montclair Cares* meeting, a group of parents, teachers, administrators, and activists who were working to fight some of the initiatives in their district. My first meeting sparked the idea that I should begin to attend the Board meetings in my own town and question why they were insisting on subjecting the children to hours upon hours of standardized tests. This was not easy for me – for some reason the public arena felt much more intimidating than the context of my classes or my professional communities, but I just could not sit back and allow my children to be tortured by these meaningless tests. I was invited to write an op-ed for a local paper on why I was refusing to let my children take the PARCC test and I began to receive calls from other reporters asking if I would respond to their questions.

My next activist step was to join Save Our Schools New Jersey (SOSNJ) which has been an amazing and inspiring community of parent activists. It is through SOSNJ that I have been educated about the ways that decisions are made in New Jersey about testing and other education legislation. I have and will continue to testify at the State Board of Education meetings, where I have voiced my concerns about using standardized tests as a high school graduation requirement for both my children in Verona, and also the students of Newark where I do much of my work. Even Griffin has gone to testify in front of the State Board. This has been an incredibly empowering experience, but I realize the value of being a parent activist within a collective. In many ways that is really a Playhouse ideal – to be part of a cooperative, to share the same values, to work toward the same goals, and to listen, respect, and empathize with others. My parent activism began at Playhouse, but even now almost nine years later, it is still very much a part of my identity.

Final Thoughts

I do not think there is a person, parent or child, who was involved at Playhouse who did not feel touched by it. It is that kind of a place where you are accepted and nurtured however you enter. I think Jeanne explains it best in a video that was made to promote the school several years back:

I have an insatiable curiosity of what makes people tick, big people and little people, and I always felt that when I put my emphasis on why is this happening, what is underneath it, looking for some kind of root instead of just treating a symptom, I felt I was able to work with it in a positive way. What I think a teacher does is sow seeds into children that they're working with. You plant the seeds, and you nurture them, and if you create the right environment, a healthy environment, they'll grow. The greatest influence that a teacher can make in a child is making the child feel like a worthwhile person. It's developing a self-image. Once you do that, if you're successful with that, the child is able to handle himself in different situations with different people at different times. It is so strong, the sense of one's self and self-identity, and feeling good about oneself is so powerful that the child can handle himself no matter what he has to face in his later, growing up years. I feel that strongly, I think that's the key.

Again and again, repeatedly I see children who have gone through Playhouse, who in later years I see the same basic approach to other people, to themselves. There's a core that stays with them. You see it when the child is 2, 3, and so how you accept it and if necessary redirect a little and nurture that depends on what kind of an adult you're going to have. Many of us are still uncomfortable with those with special difficulties, and I think that the exposure and seeing the sameness in these children [is important]. They may have difficulties, but they're still children first, and they have many of the same feelings and emotions and loves as everyone doe. So you bring into play that there are similarities and there are differences, and they're both good. But it's respecting what the person is that's most important.

I've always been somewhat of a dreamer, and I envision the future of having a beautiful building with three wings, one for young children, one for senior citizens, and one for artists in residence. And I think those three parts of the population would work so well together in enriching each other's lives. Not just one but each one would act positively on the next. I see that as a wonderful three ring … not a circus … a three-ring reality.

Since I began writing this book, we have entered into very troubling and uncertain times. Whether the onslaught of standardized testing and the detrimental impact of those tests and the ways that they influence curriculum, time in the classroom, and teaching, or the recent political environment with a president who clearly endorses racism, sexism, homophobia, xenophobia, and islamophobia, the ground is shifting and now more than ever.

We, both parents and children, need communities where we can develop positive self-concepts, take up a stance of empathy and acceptance of others, and use these principles to become critical thinkers and activists. We do not have the luxury of being passive and neither do our children. We need to resist, speak out, and act, and that takes the sort of foundation that Playhouse provided for my children and me. We need to be radicals and have radical hope, radical ideals, and radical drive. We need to be encouraged to join educational communities like Playhouse and we need to find ways to replicate Playhouse in public schools and community centers.

The Playhouse way is for all children, of all ages. It is a basic human right – to think for themselves, be true to themselves, to find their own voices, and to empathize and listen to others.

The Playhouse way is also for all parents. Again it is a basic human right – to have the opportunity to learn alongside one's child, to parent in an inquiry based way, and to be part of a cooperative community.

We have lost our way both in this country and abroad, but places like Playhouse exist to remind us to hope and to act!

REFERENCES

Ayers, W. (2004). *Teaching toward freedom: Moral commitment and ethical action in the classroom.* Boston, MA: Beacon Press.

Baruch, D. (1939). *Parents and children go to school: Adventuring in nursery school and kindergarten.* Glenview, IL: Scott Foresman and Company.

Chua, A. (2011). *Battle hymn of the tiger mom.* New York: Penguin Group.

Crawford-Seeger, R. (1948). *American folk songs for children.* New York: Double Day and Company.

De Paola, T. (1986). *My first Chanukah.* New York: Grosset and Dunlap.

Derman-Sparks, L. (1995). How well are we nurturing racial and ethnic diversity? In D. Levine, R. Lowe, B. Peterson, and R. Tenorio (Eds.), *Rethinking schools: An agenda for change,* 17-22. New York: The New Press.

Dewey, J. (1943). *The child and the curriculum* and *The school and society.* Chicago: University of Chicago Press.

Dewey, J. (1938). *Experience and education.* New York: Macmillan.

Diaz, J. (2016). Under President Trump radical hope is our best weapon. *The New Yorker,* November 21. http://www.newyorker.com/magazine/2016/11/21/under-president-trump-radical-hope-is-our-best-weapon

Doherty, G., Firth, C., Buirski, N., Green, S., Turtletaub, M., & Saraf, P. (Producers), & Nichols, J. (Director). (2016). *Loving* [Motion picture]. UK/ USA: Focus Features.

Erickson, E. H. (1951). A healthy personality in every child. *Digest of the fact-finding report of the midcentury White House Conference on Children and Youth, Washington D.C.* Raleigh, NC: Health Publications Institute.

Fine, E. (2015). *Raising peacemakers.* New York: Garn Press.

Friedan, B. (1963). *The feminine mystique.* New York: W. W. Norton and Company.

Gesell, A., & Ilg, F. L. (1949). *Child development: An introduction to the study of human growth.* New York: Harper.

Goodman, Y. M. (1996). Kidwatching: An alternative to testing. In S. Wilde (Ed.), *Notes from a kidwatcher: Selected writings of Yetta M. Goodman,* 211-227. Portsmouth, NH: Heinemann.

Guthrie, W. & U. S. Coast Guard Band, N. L. (1945). *This Land Is Your Land.* MENC. [Audio] Retrieved from the Library of Congress, https://www.loc.gov/item/ihas.100010446

Hewes, D. W. (1998). *It's the camaraderie: A history of parent cooperative schools.* Davis, CA. Center for Cooperatives, University of California.

Hymes, Jr., J. L. (1968). *Teaching the child under six.* Columbus, OH: Charles E. Merrill Publishing Company.

Hymes, Jr., J. L. (1949). *Being a good parent.* New York: Teacher

College Press.

Kohn, A. (2015). Let the Kids Learn Through Play. *The New York Times Sunday Review* (May 16th, 2015). http://www.nytimes.com/2015/05/17/opinion/sunday/let-the-kids-learn-through-play.html

Lear, J. (2008). *Radical hope: Ethics in the face of cultural devastation.* Cambridge, MA: Harvard University Press.

Lloyd, W. A., & Rice, T. (1982). *Joseph and the amazing technicolor dreamcoat.* London: Pavilion Books in association with M. Joseph.

London School of Hygiene and Tropical Medicine. (2016). Young gay, bisexual men six times more likely to attempt suicide than older counterparts. https://www.sciencedaily.com/releases/2016/04/160426215435.htm

Moll, L. C., Amanti, C., Neff, D., & Gonzalez, N. (1992). Funds of knowledge for teaching: Using a qualitative approach to connect homes and classroom. *Theory into Practice, 31*(2), 132-141.

Moorman, M. (1994). *Light the lights: A story about celebrating Hanukkah and Christmas.* New York: Cartwheel books.

Muncy, R. (2004). Cooperative motherhood and democratic civic culture in postwar suburbia, 1940-1965. *Journal of Social History* 38(2), 285-310.

Nelson, S. (2016). *First do no harm: Progressive education in a time of existential risk.* New York: Garn Press.

Noddings, N. (1992). *The challenge to care in schools.* New York: Teachers College Press.

Obama, B. (2014). https://obamawhitehouse.archives.gov/the-press-office/2014/01/28/statement-president-passing-pete-seeger

Orlando Nightclub Massacre. Lin-Manuel Miranda Highlights Orlando as 'Hamilton' Sweeps Tonys, NBC News (June 13, 2016) http://www.nbcnews.com/storyline/orlando-nightclub-massacre/lin-manuel-miranda-s-hamilton-wins-best-musical-sweeps-tonys-n590761

Paley, V. G. (1997). Foreword. In *Starting small: Teaching tolerance in preschool and early grades* (pp. i-iii). Montgomery, AL: Teaching Tolerance Project: Southern Law Poverty Center.

PARCC http://www.parcconline.org/

Pareles, J. (2014). Pete Seeger, Songwriter and Champion of Folk Music, Dies at 94. *The New York Times* (January 28, 2014). https://www.nytimes.com/2014/01/29/arts/music/pete-seeger-songwriter-and-champion-of-folk-music-dies-at-94.html

Playhouse School. (2006). *Pillars of Playhouse.*

Pratt, C. (1947). *I learn from children: An adventure in progressive education.* New York: Harper and Row.

Race to Nowhere. (2010). Abeles, V., Congdon, J., Attia, M. Lafayette. CA: Reel Link Films.

Rethinking Schools. (1995). Taking multicultural, anti-racist education seriously: An interview with Enid Lee. In D. Levine, R. Lowe, B. Peterson, and R. Tenorio (Eds.), *Rethinking schools: An agenda for change*, 9-16. New York: The New Press.

Save Our Schools New Jersey SOSNJ http://www.saveourschoolsnj.org

Seeger, P. (2014) 14 Quotes From Pete Seeger To Help Remember His Legacy http://wcbsfm.cbslocal.com/top-lists/14-quotes-from-pete-seeger-to-help-remember-his-legacy/

Short, K., Harste, J. with Burke, C. (1996). *Creating classrooms for authors and inquirers.* Portsmouth, NH: Heinemann.

Sizer, N. (2004). Learning: Turning less into more. In D. Meier, T. R. Sizer, & N. F. Sizer, *Keeping schools: Letters to families from principals of two small schools,* 3-14. Boston: Beacon Press.

Taylor, K. W. (1967). *Parents and children learn together.* New York: Teachers College Press.

Taylor, K. W. (1954). *Parent cooperative nursery schools.* New York: Teachers College Press.

Vasquez, V. (2004). *Negotiating critical literacies with young children.* New York: Routledge Press.

Waiting for "Superman". (2011). Guggenheim, D., Kimball, B., Chilcott, L., Strickland, B., Canada, G., Rhee, M., Weingarten, R. Hollywood, CA: Paramount Home Entertainment.

ABOUT MONICA TAYLOR

Monica Taylor is an urban teacher educator, social justice advocate, and parent activist. She is currently a professor and deputy chair of the Department of Secondary and Special Education at Montclair State University.

Over the past 27 years, she has taught in an alternative middle school in NYC, worked with adolescent women Crips as they negotiated their multiple identities, parented two sons, and more recently co-led the math/science cohort of the Newark Montclair Urban Teacher Residency. She is co-Principal Investigator of the Wipro Science Education Fellows grant which supports science teacher leaders in five districts in New Jersey.

She has several publications on teaching for social justice, urban teacher education, and the self-study of teacher education practices. Her most recent book, co-written with Emily J. Klein, is *A year in the life of a third space urban teacher residency: Using inquiry to reinvent teacher education.*

Her commitments to social justice manifest in all aspects of her life. She advocates for her own children as well as New Jersey students as an organizer for Save Our Schools NJ. She also deeply values the work of the many teachers with whom she is in contact.

Made in the USA
Middletown, DE
16 September 2017